D1035932

H. G. WELLS
IN
LOVE

Autobiographical works by H.G. Wells

EXPERIMENT IN AUTOBIOGRAPHY, 2 vols.

H. G. WELLS IN LOVE (edited by G. P. Wells)

H. G. WELLS
IN
LOVE

POSTSCRIPT TO AN EXPERIMENT IN AUTOBIOGRAPHY

EDITED BY
G. P. WELLS

LITTLE, BROWN AND COMPANY · BOSTON · TORONTO

LIBRARY OF CONGRESS CATALOG CARD NO. 84-81814

FIRST AMERICAN EDITION

PRINTED IN THE UNITED STATES OF AMERICA

This particular brain ... has arrived at the establishment of the Socialist World-State as its directive purpose and has made that its religion and end.

Other systems of feeling and motive run across or with or against the main theme. . . . I suspect the sexual system should be at least the second theme, when it is not the first, in every autobiography, honestly and fully told.

H. G. Wells, *Experiment in Autobiography*

CONTENTS

Chapter the Second

THE LAST PHASE

LIST OF ILLUSTRATIONS

between pages 96 *and* 97

ACKNOWLEDGEMENTS

The editor and the publisher wish to thank the following for their help and generosity in providing illustrations for this volume: Dr Martin Wells, Mrs Bernard Alexander, the Mansell Collection, Virago Press Limited, the Council and Librarian of Newnham College, Cambridge, the British Broadcasting Corporation.

Photograph credits: 5 Marcel Sternberger, 16 Lambert Weston, 17 J. Russell & Son, 20 Howard Coster, 21, 24, 25 Virago Press Ltd, 22 E. A. Hoppé, The Mansell Collection, 23 Newnham College, 29 Anthony Whelan, 30 BBC. The original source of illustration 26 is unknown; the photograph is reproduced here from *The Time Traveller* by Norman and Jeanne Mackenzie (Weidenfeld & Nicolson, 1973) by kind permission of Weidenfeld & Nicolson Ltd.

H. G. WELLS
IN
LOVE

EXPLANATION OF THIS VOLUME

My father's autobiography, titled *Experiment in Autobiography*, appeared in 1934 when he was sixty-eight years old. Fifty years later comes the present volume, *H.G. Wells in Love*, extending and completing the earlier work.

For reasons at which the reader can guess, he said little in *Experiment in Autobiography* about his many love affairs, although some of them were of great importance to him. Shortly after the appearance of that work he began to write another, titled *Postscript to an Experiment in Autobiography* and subtitled "On Loves and the Lover-Shadow," in which he described and analysed the chief of them. This *Postscript*, here published for the first time, is the most substantial part of *H.G. Wells in Love*.

But first, at his posthumous command, is an "Introduction" which he wrote in 1928 to *The Book of Catherine Wells*. That book was a collection of my mother's writings, most of them not previously published, which he assembled as a memorial to her shortly after she died. Abundant detail about their life together is to be found in *Experiment in Autobiography*. In this vivid "Introduction" he concentrates the essence of their relationship. It is indeed required reading—posthumously required—for anybody who wants to understand *Postscript to an Experiment in Autobiography* which follows it here.[1]

"She stuck to me so sturdily that in the end I stuck to myself." So he writes of Catherine Wells in his "Introduction," "I do not know what I should have been without her. She

[1] See "About the Publication of this Postscript", p. 234.

stabilized my life. She gave it a home and dignity. She preserved its continuity." All this in spite of his many love affairs in her lifetime. And after she died of cancer in October 1927 he found himself confused, unprotected, adrift. "I want peace for work. I am distressed by immediate circumstances. My thought and work are encumbered by claims and vexations and I cannot see any hope of release from them; any hope of a period of serene and beneficent activity, before I am overtaken altogether by infirmity and death. . . . I am putting even the pretence of work aside in an attempt to deal with this situation. I am writing a report about it—to myself." He wrote these words in 1932, "one wakeful night, somewhen between two and five in the early morning," and two years later the report had grown into *Experiment in Autobiography*.

He had achieved re-integration, partly by proclaiming the service of a future world-state as the central purpose of his life and partly by falling (or throwing himself) head over heels in love with Moura Budberg, and persuading himself that she would make him a brilliant wife and give him the support he so badly needed.

But Moura was unaccountably reluctant to marry him. Suddenly he was disillusioned, as he tells in the *Postscript*, by a few unguarded remarks at a party in Moscow in July 1934, and so "in an evening my splendid Moura was smashed to atoms."

The shock of disillusion was followed by a deep, nearly suicidal depression. Slowly he worked himself out of it. The self analysis involved in the writing of the *Postscript*, which he then undertook, played a major part in his recovery.

My father started writing the *Postscript* late in 1934. Having no deadline for publication, he worked on it intermittently, sometimes pressing on with it and sometimes resting it, for a matter of eight years. We may distinguish two stages in the writing of it, differing in style and aim and here shown as separate chapters.

The first, "On Loves and the Lover-Shadow," was written to supplement *Experiment in Autobiography* by filling in what was there left out. "What this Postscript deals with," he emphasized, "is not the main strand of my life but the sexual, domestic and intimate life sustaining it." But it was definitely not meant to stand alone, as his "Note about the Publication of this Postscript" makes clear.

He began by drawing up a list of section titles, hardly differing from the one in our table of contents, then wrote the text straight through (except that he occasionally looked back to revise an earlier page) until he got to the words THE END, and doubly underlined them, on May 2nd, 1935. But this was not the end of his labour. He had worked his way through thirteen of the sections in our present table of contents—for the "Looseleaf Diary" had yet to appear—plus two others enlarging on the concept of a Lover-Shadow. These two he transferred in June 1935 to another book he was writing called *The Anatomy of Frustration*, "an attempt to review and make a synthesis of life to-day."[2] He struggled for a year and a half, from May 1935 to September 1936, to organize and express his basic beliefs about human living. On the one hand he planned and wrote *The Anatomy of Frustration* and on the other he revised "On Loves and the Lover-Shadow," and especially its later sections, over and over again. The original manuscript and all of the subsequently corrected and replaced pages have

[2] *The Anatomy of Frustration* was started in May 1935 and published, after parts of it had been aired in the *Spectator*, on September 18th, 1936. Professing to give the views of a fictitious American scientist cum industrialist cum philosopher called William Burroughs Steele, it vigorously attacks the influences, in ourselves and in our society, which frustrate the forward movement of mankind towards a fuller and happier life.

been kept. They show that he revised the work a dozen times in eighteen months until, on September 18th, 1936, he wrote THE END for the last time, accompanied by a note, later deleted, "On which date I am strongly disposed to write Finis to it all."[3]

His section on "The Suicidal Mood," written in 1935, helps us to understand that note.

By this time "On Loves and the Lover-Shadow" was practically finished. He was to make retrospective alterations in later years, mostly very minor ones and nearly all of them to the closing pages of the "Moura" section, but by and large he had done what he set out to do. The work combines with *Experiment in Autobiography* to review in breadth his life up to the mid-thirties.

After that he gave his main attention to other activities. But from time to time he looked again at the *Postscript*, touching up what he had already written and also adding new matter at the end to bring his story up to date. He opened a new eleventh section, called "Looseleaf Diary," to accommodate these additions and later changed its title to "The Last Phase." I have used the two titles to separate the eleventh section as a second chapter because of its great difference, in form and in scope, from the earlier sections of the *Postscript*. "Looseleaf Diary" continues the combined work, not simply "On Loves and the Lover-Shadow," telling both of his sentimental life and also of "the story of my intellectual life as I left it in my original *Experiment in Autobiography*."

The opening sentences of "Note by Another Hand" (p. 230) were written in 1936, so he had evidently begun to think by that time of going on with the record for the rest of his days. But effectively it ends in 1942 with the waste-paper basket

[3]I believe that the existence of the *Postscript* was known to very few people other than my wife Marjorie, his secretary, who had to type it over and over again.

(p. 230). After that he added only some fragments of vituperation against a few people who had annoyed him and the rudiments of a derisive attack on contemporary universities.

My father had no intention of publishing the *Postscript* in his lifetime but he left instructions (pp. 234–5) insisting that when the time came it should be published, not by itself but bound up with *Experiment in Autobiography* and the "Introduction" to *The Book of Catherine Wells*, "so all the main masses of my experiences and reactions will fall into proportion." We have disobeyed him about binding everything together. It would have made an unwieldy book. To publish the whole in separate volumes, as we have done, allows those who already have *Experiment in Autobiography* to buy only the supplementary one. Nowhere did my father suggest a title for his proposed comprehensive volume and I have improvised *H.G. Wells in Love* for the supplement in the present compromise. It should however be noted that my title is misleading to this extent, that the full story of his two marriages, the first to his cousin, Isabel, and the second to my mother, Amy Catherine *alias* Jane, is not to be found between its covers. For this the reader must go to *Experiment in Autobiography*.

Some editing of the *Postscript* was necessary. He left three typescripts of the entire work, a top copy and two carbon copies, the top copy with a few final corrections in his own hand. There was also a mass of manuscript and discarded typescript. The top copy had been kept in old-fashioned spring-back binders and my father's revisions were made by hand on this copy; the revised pages were then discarded and replaced by fresh typescript. The discards were however preserved, so that it is possible, though toilsome, to follow the evolution of the text over the years. There were many changes, and one of the recurring problems in the preparation of the text for publication was to choose which version of a particular passage to use. I have nearly always taken the top copy as definitive. Difficulties arose when, in the 1940s, he made additions or corrections to sections written years before and especially when these involved the modification of earlier judgments. In such cases I have generally given priority to the earlier version, written while the events were relatively fresh in his mind.

I have been advised to add that I take no responsibility for the accuracy of my father's statements. My job, as I see it, has been to present what he wrote, and not to correct it. But I have direct personal knowledge of several episodes in the "Postscript" which are described rather differently in other biographies, and am sure that the versions of these here given are correct.

One or two minor deletions were felt to be desirable. A special problem was the section on "The Suicidal Mood," because he struck it out several times over the years, each time putting it back again later. His last decision was to omit the section, but I thought it too interesting, and too relevant to his story, to lose. My only major excision was his account of a long and complicated dispute with Odette Keun about her usufruct of Lou Pidou, incorporating a voluminous and sometimes fiery, sometimes obscene and sometimes libellous correspondence—around 15,000 words altogether. The dispute ran on through 1936 and 1937, after the two had parted company, and it seemed to me that its importance hardly justified so long a digression.

In considering these problems I was greatly helped by my brother and fellow trustee, Frank Wells, and since his illness and death by his son Martin and my daughter Catherine Stoye. Responsibility for the final decisions is mine.

G. P. Wells

PROLOGUE

INTRODUCTION TO

THE BOOK OF CATHERINE WELLS

§1

MY WIFE when she died had written and published a few short stories and she had collaborated with my younger son in one or two others. But what was printed was but a small part of the amount she wrote. I knew something of her writing, but not very much, because it was her desire to succeed independently of my influence. It was her desire to write and succeed as herself. Her literary activities were not due to any urgent necessity in her nature. She was not compelled to expression by any uncontrollable drive within. Indeed she was by temperament rather reserved than expressive. But living as she did in an atmosphere of continual literary activity, where statement in words as finely chosen as possible had a special importance, her natural inhibition of comment even to herself, was gradually broken down and she began to write, first, I think, to see what it was she herself was really thinking and feeling about life, and then to convey this, not perhaps to the world at large, but to some imagined closely sympathetic reader. She did not write for me, though she did her best to make me feel and to feel herself that I was not excluded. She shrank from publicity; nevertheless she began to think more and more of publication.

She sent her work to various periodicals from a different address and through various agents so as not to be identified with me. Her imaginary reader never materialized, and I think would not have been particularly welcome if he had materialized. She was seeking expression for something that she realized she herself did not completely grasp and probably she would have been violently repelled by any assurances of understanding.

This shy and withdrawn authorship of hers began quite early in her married life but it became much more extensive and deliberate in later years. She sought her own proper forms and phrasing with peculiar effort because for the first twenty years of our life together she had been accustomed to act as my secretary and typist, and so her mind had acquired many habits and prepossessions about method that she shook off with difficulty. Yet I think the reader of the pages that follow will agree with me that she did at last achieve a delicately characteristic style. She has given in this series of stories and in these scraps of verse the quality of a mood, a state of mind, a phase of personality rather intangible, inaggressive yet resistant, not forcible in any way but clear, clean, sweet and very very fine in its texture. This aspect of her personality is pervaded by a certain wistful melancholy; it is in the mood of very still landscapes, bright yet touched by the softness of evening, and pity broods upon it. Desire is there, but it is not active aggressive desire. It is a desire for beauty and sweet companionship. There is a lover, never seen, never verified, elusively at the heart of this desire. Frustration haunts this desire. And also fear is never far away, an elvish fear like the fear of a child's dream. Such is the mood in which nearly all these pieces were written. Whenever my wife sat down alone to write it is manifest that very speedily that phase of her mind returned. I doubt if it was even a prevalent phase in her complex and subtle composition. But it was rooted very deeply in her character, it must, I think, have been the normal atmosphere of her girlish reveries, and however overlaid and set aside in her actively living hours it came to the surface so soon as she was alone with herself.

I have put forth this book under the name of Catherine Wells of set intention; it was the name she used invariably in her writings, but it was not her full name (which was Amy Catherine) nor was it the name by which she was best known to her friends. I had thrust upon her and she had been ready and willing to wear for everyday use and our common purposes a congenial presentation of herself that we had christened "Jane." To most of our friends and acquaintances she was Jane and nothing else. They hardly caught a glimpse of Catherine. Jane was a person of much greater practical ability than Catherine. She was the tangible Catherine and made decisions freely, while Catherine herself stayed in the background amiably aloof. Jane ordered a house well and was an able "shopper;" she helped people in difficulties and stood no nonsense from the plumber. Her medicine cupboard at home was prepared for all occasions. She had gone through a Red Cross course so as to be competent in domestic emergencies. She had a file of shop addresses where things needed could be bought. Her garden was a continually glowing success and she was a member of the Royal Horticultural Society and kept a garden book and a diary to check and improve her methods. Every year the gardeners were packed off to the Chelsea Show. She transacted and invested for her unhelpful uncertain husband, and she was wise and wary in his affairs and a searchlight of honesty and clear but kindly illumination in his world. Nonsensical people fled her quiet eye. One particular sort of nonsensical people she had dealt with specially and reduced to orderly subjection and those were the vague race of translators and would-be translators who entangle and obscure authors in foreign lands. For them she had devised a method and a standard agreement and built up a system of relationship abroad that no literary agent could better. That was Jane.

Certainly there was such a Jane about in my life. I cannot tell how much I owe her. But indeed my wife was neither Jane, which was her working and practically developed self, nor Catherine, which was the name of her personal reverie and of her literary life. She was both of them and many more as the lights about her changed.

§2

TO RECALL the facets of this being, whose Catherine personality is presented by these fine-spirited and, to my mind, very charming writings, is to go over the tale of adventures we have had together for nearly five and thirty years. I have been more retrospective in the past six months than in all my life before. I give here a portrait of her, dating from about the time of our first meeting. That is Miss Robbins, her first facet. There one sees the person who came into the cramming classes I conducted in practical biology, for candidates for the London Bachelor of Science examinations. She was wearing mourning then for her father, who had recently been killed by accident on the railway; he had left no property worth speaking of and she was struggling to secure a degree in order to become a schoolmistress and earn a living for her mother and herself.

I thought her then a very sweet and valiant little figure indeed, with her schoolgirl satchel of books and a very old-fashioned unwieldly microscope someone had lent her, and I soon came to think her the most wonderful thing in my life. I was a crude, hard young man in those days, who had got a fairly good London University degree by way of a studentship at the Royal College of Science; I was widely but irregularly read—suggestions from Shelley and Huxley interwove with strands from Carlyle, Morris and Henry George—and my worldly and social experience was somewhere about the level of my Mr. Lewisham's. I was at war with the world and by no means sure that I should win. I held extreme religious, social and political opinions that shut me out from ordinary school-work, and I found a satisfaction in beating the regular university teachers in their own examinations. Very soon this new pupil became the embodiment of all the understanding and quality I desired in life. We talked—over our frogs and rabbits. The cramming organization for which I worked had published an expansion of my teaching notes as a *Textbook of Biology* copiously but blottesquely illustrated by myself. She drew so much more firmly and clearly than I did that I got her to redraw all my diagrams for a second edition. Our friendship grew swiftly beyond the bounds of friendship and I was amazed to find that she could care for me as much as I did for her. When I told her I had smashed a kidney at football and lost a large part of one lung, that seemed to her merely a reason for immediate action. I do not think either of us expected to live ten years. But we meant to live every minute there was for us to live. We were the most desperate of lovers; we launched ourselves upon our life together with less than fifty pounds between us and absolute disaster, and we pulled through. We never begged nor borrowed, we never cheated, and we worked and paid our way first into a position of security and then to real prosperity.

And I seem to remember now that we did it with a very great deal of gaiety.

As I look back over those early years together, I find the grave little figure in mourning, whom one auspicious afternoon I had discovered awaiting me in my laboratory, changing by the most imperceptible degrees into the companion of an easier life in a broadening world. Jane developed and Catherine began to appear. Thirty years ago we "went abroad" for the first time. It was our first holiday and a plain intimation that we were getting the upper hand in our struggle for existence. We went straight through to Rome where George Gissing had promised to show us the sights. Rome in those days was still mellow and beautiful. Afterwards we went on alone to Naples and Capri and came back by way of Florence to England. My wife could be not only the most trustworthy and active of helpers but also the most appreciative of petted companions, and on this and many other journeys work was set aside and I managed the trunks and the luggage and she beamed happily upon the subservient spectacle. We armed ourselves with sheets of the Siegfried map and went to walk in Switzerland, not to climb but seeking snowy and lonely paths. She fell in love with the Alps and we planned and carried out long tramps over the passes and down into Italy. We would slip away from our home at Folkestone for a fortnight or so, going often in June before the main holiday crowd and just as the inns were re-opening. So we found spring flowers and unspoilt smiles.

The passion for high places took hold of her. I was never much of a climber because of my restricted lung and kidney surfaces, and after the war I was no good at it at all, but then my sons were growing up and she would go with them, developing a greater ambition every year. All I saw of that side of her after the war was the triumphant snapshots she sent me. She would toil through long excursions upon foot or upon skis, never going very fast or brilliantly, but never giving up, a little indefatigable smiling figure, dusted with the snow of her not infrequent tumbles. I would write to her from among my agaves and olive orchards and she would answer from her snows, and afterwards we would trace together, upon those nice brown explicit Swiss maps, the expeditions she had made or still proposed to make.

§3

WE HAD NO CHILDREN for some years because we thought our outlook too precarious to inflict its risks upon other lives than our own. But when we had built a house for ourselves, got a thousand pounds put by and I had found an insurance company that did not regard my little misadventures with lung and kidney too pessimistically, we thought it time to launch a family. We had two sons. She fought for the life of the first of them and for her own life for more than four and twenty dreadful hours. She seemed a very little fragile thing in that battle and then it was, I fear, that the seed of her death was sown in her.

But now beside Jane and Catherine a third main strand of her personality became important. Our house became a home when the voice of that hopeful young biologist, Mr. G.P. Wells, pervaded it, and I suppose it was his practice which determined that the new aspect of my wife should be called "Mummy." But the real importance of Mummy came gradually. In the earlier years of our parentage very much of the care of our children could be entrusted to a skilful nurse and a capable governess. My wife watched over our boys' temperatures and behaviour and we met them for perhaps an hour a day, and saw to it that they learnt to speak plainly, count straight and draw freely, and liked us as play-fellows. But as they became schoolboys there developed much more companionship and intimacy between them and Mummy. They brought home their friends from school and Cambridge, and Mummy became the centre of a bright fresh world of youths and young men.

A marked characteristic of this Mummy, which neither Jane nor Catherine displayed, was considerable histrionic ability. Mummy in her later years was a most gay, inventive and amusing actress. Many of our friends must remember the funny and yet consistent little figures she could evoke; her terrible detective with one wildly glaring eye between his turned-up coat-collar and his turned-down hat; her series of venomous old ladies, from pew-openers and charwomen to duchesses, with their astonishing and convulsing asides; her queenly personages with the strangest of Victorian hats and a sublime dignity; her Mrs. Noah, murmuring her secret anxieties about "the cost of it all," and "how-*ever*" she would "keep 'em all clean;" her anxious maternal care of a succession of enormous and generally unsuitable children.

Charades had played an exhilarating rôle in our lives for many years. In the beginning we had had to fight the world very much alone; we had had few acquaintances, and fewer friends, and kept little company. We talked a lot of nonsense and had many jokes to help ourselves through those austerer days. Of that there is no telling. But as soon as we began to prosper and meet miscellaneous people, we relaxed into social play very gladly. It was in 1897 or 1898, in a little house we occupied at Sandgate, that we found congenial next-door neighbours, a Mr. Arthur Popham and his wife, with two jolly children, and a coming and going of pleasant cousins and other friends, and could for the first time "play the fool" and release our human disposition to mimicry and mockery in a roomful of people. "Dumb crambo" was the earliest form of our dramatic expression. Then for some reason we took to shadow-shows. These shadow-shows dropped out of our practice long since, but in those days they were of sufficient importance to make us stipulate, when we built ourselves Spade House at Sandgate, for an archway in the middle of a room which would give sufficient depth behind the white sheet for expanding and diminishing shadows. Afterwards we turned to charades, dumb or spoken, to impersonations of various sorts, to burlesques of current plays and to suddenly invented plays of our own. Sometimes we did scenes of travel or "moral instruction," scenes illustrating the unpleasantness of wickedness and the charms of virtue. Often we drew upon history, sacred or profane. The boys grew into a tradition of rapidly improvised drama, and took an increasingly important share in this fun, and Mummy got better at it and better.

I turn over my memories of these freakish quaint affairs, into which people threw themselves with astonishing zest. A great melodrama at Sandgate, with a Thames Embankment scene and a doped race-horse (Popham was the front half) all complete, returns to me out of the early days; Ford Madox Hueffer was the sole croupier at a green table in a marvellous Monte Carlo scene and Jane was a gambling duchess of entirely reckless habits. Then come certain travel pictures at Hampstead, with H. W. Nevinson as the most Teutonic of railway porters proclaiming the trains at the waiting-room door, and Jane as a greatly encumbered mother with an equally tiny Dolly Radford as her nurse, and a string of vast crumby bun-eating children in white socks, bare calves, straw-hats on the backs of their heads, and spades and buckets, and no end of luggage. One of these infants, I remember, was my friend E. S. P. Haynes and another was W. R. Titterton, and when at last the proper train was announced Jane brought down the house by turning to Dolly and saying, with a finger pointing to Haynes, "*You* carry Siegfried," and waiting with a testy hatred on her face for her order to be obeyed.

Sydney Olivier was always a great success with us, playing the infant Moses with touching realism to Jane's Pharaoh's Daughter, and also doing a very mighty Samson with a sheep-skin mat of hair. The present, from Philip Guedalla, of a formidable-looking iron thing for cooking griddle-cakes turned our thoughts for a time to hell. "Nancy Parsons," who is now Lady Mercy Dean, queened it among the damned and the rôle Jane invented for herself was a quietly peevish grumbler with a book of regulations and a tariff of torment, of whom the presiding fiend went in manifest horror. "But, *Sir*!" she urged, finger on the regulation in question. It was a quite new terror added to hell.

But I could fill a whole book with such memories. From first to last hundreds of people must have passed through the fires of these charades of ours. The figures crowd upon me, peeping out one behind the other, like that mighty constellation of stars, painted upon the drop-scene of the London Coliseum—Arnold Bennett, Sir Frederick Keeble, Lillah M'Carthy, Basil Dean, Noël Coward, Roger Fry as a skeleton with white paper bones on black tights, Clutton Brock as a Prussian general, Philip Snowden (his first and only dramatic appearance) very wicked as an elderly raja dealing with concession-hunters, and still more wicked in a crimson skull-cap as a pope, and Frank Hodges in a white apron and with an armful of tankards as the unscrupulous landlord of an unscrupulous inn. The late George Mair was a wonderful missionary of the less attractive kind and Frank Swinnerton a terrible man about town. Sir Harry Johnston created a marvellous Noah and Charlie Chaplin created a still more marvellous Noah on entirely different lines. But every figure I recall brings yet others with it. I cannot even name a tithe of them. And through all this tangle of cheery burlesque goes my wife, gravely radiant and indefatigable. She had accumulated presses full of gaily coloured "dressing-up" garments and her instinct for effect was unerring.

All this charade business she made at last entirely hers. At first I suppose I supplied some initiatives, but she was so much more full and thorough about it, and my boys brought such enthusiasm into it, that gradually I dropped out of any share in the management and became a delighted spectator. I could never tell what odd little novelty she had plotted when she came on. She never lost the gift of surprising me into laughter and admiration. I cannot say how completely I feel now that this quaint and various volume of happy nonsense has closed for me for ever.

It has closed for ever because it was her life so much more than mine. The old place may continue as the home of a new generation, but for me now it is no more than a nest of memories. I could write on, in the same tone of happy reminiscence, of a score of other aspects of that home life she created and which was so distinctively hers. Charades were after all only the typical fun of a great variety of kindred relaxations. She had a passion for improvised dancing, and we had a big barn to dance in; and she and my boys produced several plays in the village theatre. Our week-ends would gather the most incongruous people; they would arrive on Saturday afternoon a little aloof and distrustful of one another; they would depart on Monday magically fused, having "dressed up," danced, acted, walked, played and helped get the Sunday supper. She never dominated, but she pervaded the place with such a sense of good-will, such an unqualified ardour for happiness, that the coldest warmed and the stiffest relaxed.

All that was in the normal order of things less than a year ago. I recall the bright atmosphere of coming and going, the variety of visitors about the tea-tables in the garden-house, the lit windows at night sending out shafts of acid green light upon the lawns and bushes, the warmth of movement and laughter. The curtain has come down on all that pleasant scene and never more shall I revive it. It has gone now as far beyond recall as our first shy talks in my smaller classroom at Red Lion Square or our valiant struggles up the steep passes to which the exciting zigzags of the Siegfried map had lured us.

"What fun we have had!" wrote one old friend, and that must be the epitaph upon her social self.

§4

WITH ALL THIS, I realize, I am telling little that is essential about my wife. I am writing about facets—of this aspect and of that aspect she presented to the world. I am skirting round a personality which was in its intimacy extraordinarily shy and elusive. Jane Wells and "Mummy" and the mistress of Easton Glebe were known to scores of friends, but my knowledge went deeper. There was something behind these smiling masks that Catherine Wells was seeking to express, and did at last in some of these brief pieces express very perfectly. In the silent light of the reading-lamp, writing what might never be printed, she could search for her very self.

I have told of how we two defied the current wisdom of the world and won, with Shelley and Huxley and a profound contempt for the timidities and hypocrisies of the time among our common inspirations. What is more difficult to tell is our slow discovery of the profoundest temperamental differences between us and of the problems these differences created for us. Fundamental to my wife's nature was a passion for happiness and lovely things. She was before everything else gentle and sweet. She worshipped beauty. For her, beauty was something very definite, a precious jewel to be discovered and treasured. For me beauty is incidental, so surely a part of things that one need not be directly concerned about it. I am a far less stable creature than she was, with a driving quality that holds my instabilities together. I have more drive than strength, and little patience; I am hasty and incompetent about much of the detailed business of life because I put too large a proportion of my available will and energy into issues that dominate me. Only in that way do I seem able to get on with these issues that dominate me. I have to overwork—with all the penalties of overworking in loss of grace and finish—to get my work done. In all this we were in the completest contrast and inevitably we strained against each other.

I think that young people nowadays must get a very considerable help in their adjustments from the suggestions of modern psychological science. Its analysis of motive and behaviour makes enormously for understanding and charity. But in our time psychology was still mainly a shallow and unserviceable intellectualism. We had to work out our common problem very largely by the light nature had given us. And I am appalled to reflect how much of the patience, courage and sacrifice of our compromises came from her. Never once do I remember her romancing a situation into false issues. We had two important things in our favour; first that we had a common detestation not only of falsehood but of falsity; and, secondly, that we had the sincerest affection and respect for each other. There again the feat was hers. It was an easy thing for me to keep my faith in her sense of fair-play and her perfect generosity. She never told a lie. To the end I would have taken her word against all other witnesses in the world. But she managed to sustain her belief that I was worth living for, and that was a harder task, while I made my way through a tangle of moods and impulses that were quite outside her instinctive sympathy. She stuck to me so sturdily that in the end I stuck to myself. I do not know what I should have been without her. She stabilized my life. She gave it a home and dignity. She preserved its continuity. Not without incessant watchfulness and toil. I have a hundred memories of an indefatigable typist carrying on her work in spite of a back-ache; of a grave judicial proof-reader in a garden shelter, determined that no slovenliness should escape her; of a resolute little person, clear-headed but untrained in business method, battling steadfastly with the perplexities of our accumulating accounts and keeping her grip on them.

Our temperamental differences were reflected in our convictions. Though she helped and sustained me with her utmost strength and loyalty, I do not think she believed very strongly in my beliefs. She accepted them, but she could have done without them. I am extravagantly obsessed by the thing that might be, and impatient with the present; I want to go ahead of Father Time with a scythe of my own; I have a faith in human possibilities which has become the core of my life; but she was much more acquiescent and attentive to the thing that is. She was more realist than I am and less creative. She was more aware of the loveliness of things and the sorrowfulness and cruelty in things. She admired more than I did; she kept and cherished more than I did, and she pitied much more than I did. Her philosophy was more stoical than mine, because she could neither hope nor be angry in my fashion. And when that is understood, then I think you have the key to the feeling of wistful loveliness that touches such stories here as "The Emerald," "The Beautiful House" and "The Fugitives," with their peculiar beauty.

Pity and habitual helpfulness were very characteristic of her. She was watchful for the feelings and humiliations and perplexities of everyone about her. She was alive to the discomforts caused by neglected teeth or troublesome minor ailments to poor people, and she would seize every opportunity of having matters put right for them. The timely good dentist or the timely good oculist may change a faltering life to a happy and successful one, and more than once or twice she saw that it did. And she would think of agreeable presents—a small motor-car, a gramophone, a pianola—for households where these particular things were just inaccessible. She became a very skilful giver of presents; a timely holiday for a fagged worker, a new dress for someone confronted by a social demand. She was always trying to find the perfect present that would help deaf people, but that is still to be invented. After the war we produced a book, *The Outline of History*. We did not expect it to be a profitable book, but we felt it had to be done, and there was no one in sight to do it. We were not particularly equipped for the task and it meant huge toil for both of us. We would work at Easton long after midnight, making notes from piles of books or writing up and typing notes. But this task turned out far more profitable to us than anyone could have dreamt. I do not think my wife ever thought for a moment of any personal use to be made of this enrichment. She liked people in a cheerful mood and a pleasant receptive home, but she had no trace of social ambition in her nature. She liked pretty clothes—and sometimes pretty clothes are costly—but she lacked entirely the instinct for display. She had hardly any jewels and never wanted any. But now that we really had surplus funds she made her obscure and tender benefactions more systematic. Probably of very many of them I know nothing, for we kept our money in a common account, and the administration was completely in her hands. She would consult me about any expenditure that was "serious," but not about smaller things when she felt sure I would approve. And moreover, for occasions when my harder heart might not be in agreement, she had a fund of her own.

Pity, generosity, the love of beautiful things, of noble thoughts and liberal actions! How fine she was in the unobtrusive silences of her nature! And above all she had courage. It was destined to be tested to the utmost. For five months of gathering discomfort she faced an inevitable death and her heart did not fail her.

§5

DEATH we had to watch drawing nearer to her for five months, but the first intimation of that grim advance came to us as an absolute surprise. We had always thought that things would be the other way about; that I was more likely to die first and perhaps unexpectedly. So we had arranged our affairs as far as possible to ease the blow of my withdrawal. Our home at Easton was so contrived that if instead of one of my frequent absences—for every winter for some time I have gone abroad after the sunshine—there came an absence with no end to it, everything would go on, as it had always gone on. In January of this last year she was with our youngest son and his betrothed at Arosa and I was in the easier air of the Riviera. In March we were together in Paris for a pleasant week—when I gave a lecture at the Sorbonne and such charming people as Madame Curie and Professor Perrin made much of her. She had looked forward to that visit and it was characteristic of her that she secretly took a course of lessons to revive her French before coming and so surprised everyone by her fluency. We came back to London and she seemed a little out of sorts. Neither of us thought that there was anything seriously wrong with her. I went abroad again for a motoring holiday, but before I left I made her promise to see a doctor.

My elder son departed to France also, on his honeymoon. We came back post-haste to the telegram of my younger son. She had gone through an exploratory operation without letting me know anything of its nature and the surgeons had discovered that she had inoperable cancer, very far gone and diffused, that left her hardly six months more to live.

She knew that quite clearly when I returned to her. She had questioned the doctors and obliged them to tell her. Seeing that they seemed sorry, they told me, she did her best to comfort them. "I know you cannot help it," she said. "There is nothing for you to be unhappy about."

We tried a foolish X-ray cure of which the least said the better. Then we sat down to make the best of life before the shadow reached her. And so clear and steadfast was her mind that we did contrive to win interest and happiness out of a great proportion of those hundred and fifty days. At first we hoped for a considerable recovery of strength but she never really got over the exhaustion caused by the X-ray while she was still weakened by her operation. For a few weeks she could walk up and down stairs at Easton, but then she had to be carried in a chair. We found a wonderful chair for out-of-doors, with big wheels with pneumatic tyres and good springs, and in this she could go quite considerable distances—into my neighbour's gardens at Easton Lodge and about the Park. For a time she could endure a well-sprung car and we paid a round of calls upon our friends and even went off for some days to an hotel at Felixstowe, when she had a craving to see the sea. The garden she had made at Easton flowered to perfection. The friends she cared for came to see her and she would hold a kind of reception on the tennis-courts and laugh and applaud.

She read abundantly and we got a lot out of music, bringing all the resources of the gramophone world to her. Some of the new records are marvellously delicate and expressive. We would sit about together in the sunshine listening to Beethoven, Bach, Purcell and Mozart, and later, as she grew weaker and less capable of sustained attention, we would sit side by side in silence in the dusk and find loveliness and interest in watching a newly lit wood fire burn up from the first blue flickerings.

She put all her affairs in order clearly and methodically. Day by day she weakened, but her mind never lost its integrity. It is one of the dreadful possibilities of such an illness that the increasing poison in the blood poisons the mind so that it is afflicted with strange fears and unnatural hostilities, and for that last horror I tried to prepare my mind. Nothing of that sort darkened those last days. But the lucid times contracted. More and more of the twenty-four hours was taken up in sleep and drugged endurance.

At first, she would be very gay at her breakfast when I went in to her, and the nurses would have her about in the garden by eleven or so. Then came a time when she began the day by coming down to lunch and slept through the afternoon, and had only between tea-time and bed-time for animation. She wasted and became very thin, but with a strange emaciated prettiness that somehow recalled her girlish face. She shrank to be a very little thing indeed. She was sedulous not to look haggard or dreadful or be in any way distressing to those who saw her. She spent an hour or more with her hairdresser from London within a month of her death, having her still pretty hair waved and put in order. She dressed with care until she could dress no longer.

To the very last she "carried on." She was ordering new roses to replace some that had failed in her garden within a fortnight of the end. On September the 24th she had a tree felled that darkened the servants' bedrooms, and watched the felling. It was her last time in the garden. I was not there; I had gone to London to fetch a specialist from Paris who might add, I thought, to her comfort. The nurses told me that when the tree crashed she turned away and would not look.

A great weariness crept upon her. She became more and more ready for the night, when an opiate put her into a contented sleep. She liked life still, but with a relaxing hold. She told me she was ready now to sleep for ever. She was very anxious I should not grieve for her and that I should feel sure I had made her happy. One thing held her still to life. She was very fond of our younger son Frank and the sweetheart he had chosen in his undergraduate days, and she wanted to see them married. The three of them had spent some cheerful times together in Switzerland and Italy. She ordered a wedding-breakfast for the occasion. She would not let anyone else do that. She could not come to the church but she hoped she might be carried down to sit at table. It was to be upon the seventh of October. The date reminded her of the birthday of a little niece and a present she had bought for her in the

Burlington Arcade and stowed away. She had that hunted out and sent off. Then, on the sixth she began to sink very rapidly. She lay still and we thought she was insensible. But she heard the sound of my son's car as it came under her window on the way to the garage. He had come back from his work in London for his wedding on the morrow. She had been waiting for that familiar sound. She revived. She knew him and her weak caress fluttered over him and she said something indistinct to him about the wedding. Then her attention faded out. She spoke no more, she became a breathing body from which all token of recognition had departed, and an hour or so later, with her unresponsive hand in mine, she ceased to breathe.

The wedding seemed so much the completion of her life that we resolved to carry it out. We changed the hour from eleven to nine so as to avoid any gathering of people. We drove down through the morning sunshine to the old parish church of Dunmow to meet the bride and her parents, and after the ceremony the two young people went off together into the world and I and my elder son and his wife returned to our home.

The white and purple Michaelmas daisies were glorious that October morning. It seemed incredible that I could not take in a great armful for her to see.

§6

AMONG THE LAST WISHES she scribbled in a little memorandum book a few days before her death, she wrote very distinctly, "I desire that my body be cremated," and signed it with a resolute flourish. I think she feared there might be some legal impediment unless her own words could be produced.

Circumstances conspired to make that last scene a very

beautiful one. I had dreaded it greatly, for I have few memories of such services that are not touched with something bleak and hard. I had to set about finding a secular form for the occasion if my mind was not to be offended once again by the Corinthian clevernesses of St. Paul, which constitute the substance of the standard Anglican ceremony. I consulted Dr. Hayward and he gave me a little book of funeral addresses prepared by F.J. Gould. One of those I chose, and then began to alter. In the end I altered it greatly. I altered it, not because I thought I could improve it, but because I kept finding some new way of fitting it more closely to this special occasion. I wrote in it and wrote upon it until at last hardly anything was left of it except certain quotations and the general shape. It became almost entirely a personal testimony, and these quotations and the reflections associated with them stand out in it like a portion of some preceding building incorporated, but not completely identified, in a new edifice.

Dr. T.E. Page read this address. He sat at a desk facing the little grey coffin from which all the flowers and wreaths had been removed and piled aside, and he read very clearly and well to a considerable gathering of our friends. We had circulated her expressed wish that no mourning should be worn for her, and so all these kind and friendly and sorrowful people came exactly themselves and not odd and disguised in unfamiliar black. It made the assembly much more intimate and touching. There were old associates and friends to recall every stage in our five and thirty years together, and many must have taken pains to come and have set other things aside, for the notice given had been very short.

We stood while Mr. Reginald Paul, who was the organist on this occasion, played César Franck's *Pièce Héroïque* and then we seated ourselves and Dr. Page read these words:

"We have come together in this chapel to-day to greet

for the last time our very dear friend, Catherine Wells.

"We meet in great sadness, for her death came in the middle season of her life when we could all have hoped for many more years of her brave and sweet presence among us. She died a victim of cancer, that still unconquered enemy of human happiness. For months her strength faded, but not her courage nor her kindness. To the end she faced her destiny with serenity and with a gentle unfailing smile for those who ministered to her.

"It would be foolish to pretend that this event does not bring home to us very vividly a sense of the extreme brevity of life for all mankind. The days of man 'are as grass,' said the Psalmist; and again, 'The days of our years are threescore years and ten, and though men be so strong that they come to fourscore years, yet is their strength then but labour and sorrow; so soon passeth it away and we are gone.' Nevertheless we may learn from such lives as this that a precious use can be made of brief days and that the courage of a loving Stoicism is proof against despair.

"This was a life freed from all supernatural terrors and superstitious illusions. To-day few are troubled by evil imaginations of what may lie beyond this peace and silence that has come upon our friend. This dear career is now like a task accomplished, a tale of years lived bravely and generously and gone now beyond reach of any corruption. And though the dark shadow of her interruption and cessation lies athwart our minds to-day, it is a shadow out of which we can pass. We can think of the worth of such living as hers gladly even in the face of death. There is much wisdom and comfort for us in these words of Spinoza's: 'The free man thinks of nothing so little as of death and his wisdom is a meditation not upon death but upon life.'

"The city of the living world is a perennial city, founded

deep in the immemorial past and towering up in the future to heights beyond our vision, its walls fashioned like a mosaic out of lives such as this one. It could not be and its hope could not be, except for the soundness and rightness of such lives. All brave lives have been lived for ever. The world of human achievement exists in them and through them; in them it has its being and its hope, and in it also they continue, deathless, a perpetual conquest over the grave and over the sting of death.

"Some lives stand out upon headlands and are beacons for all mankind. But some, more lovely and more precious, shine in narrower places and come only by chance gleams and reflections to the knowledge of the outer world. So it was with our friend. The best and sweetest of her is known only to one or two of us: subtle and secret, it can never be told. Faithful, gentle, wise, and self-forgetful, she upheld another who mourns her here to-day: to him she gave her heart and her youth and the best of her brave life, through good report and evil report and the stresses and mischances of our difficult and adventurous world. She was a noble wife, a happy mother, and the maker of a free and kindly and hospitable home. She was perhaps too delicately inaggressive for wide and abundant friendships, but her benevolence was widespread and incessant. She watched to seize opportunities for unobtrusive good deeds. No one could give the full record of her tender half-apologetic gifts, her generous help, her many benefactions, for no one knows them all. She thought that a good deed talked about or even held in memory lost half its worth. She was great-minded. She could forgive ingratitude and bore no resentment for a slight. Never was a single word of ungracious judgment passed by her. 'Poor dears,' she would say, 'Poor silly dears,' when some ugly story or the report of some vindictive quarrel came to her, for it seemed to her that evil acts must be painful and shameful even to the doer. She was a fountain of pity and mercy, except to herself. For herself she was ever exacting. Truth was in her texture; never did she tell a lie nor do any underhand act. She had a great affection for beautiful and graceful things, and her taste seemed to grow finer with the years. Of natural things she most loved the roses of her cherished garden and sunlight upon mountain snows. . . .

"No more will she see the flowers and the sun, and the pain and increasing weakness of these last months also are at an end for her; but the spirit of her life lives with us still, she is still among us, a spirit of pity and kindness, honour and merciful integrity, in the memories of all who knew her.

"And now her dear body must pass from our sight towards the consuming flames. Her life was a star, fire goes to fire and light to light. She returns to the furnace of material things from which her life was drawn. But within our hearts she rests enshrined and, in the woven fabric of things accomplished, she lives for ever."

Here the reader paused and the coffin passed slowly through the doors leading to the furnace chamber. As it did so all the congregation stood and remained standing. The doors closed and the voice of the reader resumed:

"We have committed our beloved to the flames and soon there will be but a few ashes, as a relic of the form we knew and loved.

"And as we stand here, we whose bodies must presently follow hers into that same peace and that same dispersal, let us think for a moment of the use or the misuse we may make of the time that yet remains for us.

"And may the memory of this gentle starry spirit be a

talisman to hold us to charity, faithfulness, and generosity of living."

The reading ceased. The great arch of the crematorium chapel was open upon a wide space of garden glowing with flowers in the serene sunshine of a perfect October afternoon. The stillness of everything outside gave it an air of expectation. As one close friend of hers said to me, it was as though at any moment she might have come in upon us with her garden-basket and those red-handled shears of hers upon her arm, smiling as she was wont to smile. When the last words of the address had been pronounced, Mr. Paul played Bach's *Passacaglia*, a piece she had greatly loved.

I should have made no attempt to follow the coffin had not Bernard Shaw, who was standing next to me, said: "Take the boys and go behind. It's beautiful."

When I seemed to hesitate he whispered: "I saw my mother burnt there. You'll be glad if you go."

That was a wise counsel and I am very grateful for it. I beckoned to my two sons and we went together to the furnace room. The little coffin lay on a carriage outside the furnace doors. These opened. Inside one saw an oblong chamber whose fire-brick walls glowed with a dull red heat. The coffin was pushed slowly into the chamber and then in a moment or so a fringe of tongues of flame began to dance along its further edges and spread very rapidly. Then in another second the whole coffin was pouring out white fire. The doors of the furnace closed slowly upon that incandescence.

It was indeed very beautiful. I wished she could have known of those quivering bright first flames, so clear they were and so like eager yet kindly living things.

I have always found the return from a burial a disagreeable experience, because of the pursuing thought of that poor body left behind boxed up in the cold wet ground and waiting the coming of the twilight. But Jane, I felt, had gone clean out of life and left nothing to moulder and defile the world. So she would have had it. It was good to think she had gone as a spirit should go.

POSTSCRIPT
TO AN
EXPERIMENT IN AUTOBIOGRAPHY

CHAPTER THE FIRST

ON LOVES AND THE LOVER-SHADOW

§1
The Lover-Shadow

In the book I have called *Experiment in Autobiography*, I tried to trace out the emotional development of a human brain from the year of my birth in 1866 to the year 1934. It was a rather quick and bold type of brain, as I conceived it, but its general texture was mediocre, and it served rather as a sample of the current movement of thought and purpose during that period of human experience than as anything extraordinary in itself. Some critics said that my assertion of its essential mediocrity was insincere and were inclined to overrate my quality and blame me for a sort of inverted arrogance. But I meant exactly what I said; it was a very typical common brain. Its one outstanding quality was a disposition to straightforwardness. I told as fully as I could of the sexual awakening of this brain, of its primary emotional and sentimental reactions, and of the play of its instinctive impulses amidst established conventions of behaviour, up to the establishment of what I called a *modus vivendi* between husband and wife, towards 1900. Thereafter sexual events and personal intimacies had to fall into the background of the story. They were no longer of primary formative importance, and it was possible to make the development of a modern ideology the dominant topic of the later chapters. But I regretted the dimming of the easy frankness of the beginning. These later personal affairs were of considerable importance; significant sexual and personal intimacies occurred after 1900—a thing I made quite apparent in general terms at least—and the omission of any particular discussion of them caused, as it were, an effect of a partial blankness within the general outline.

The main reason for this suppression was, of course, that a number of people who were still living in 1934 were bound to be affected very seriously by a public analysis of the rôles they played in my life. And it seems to me that the only way to round off my attempt to give the material facts of a complete brain story is to write down the broad facts of these imaginative and emotional complications that have been suppressed in the narrative, here and now, and leave the record to be published at some later date when this practical objection will have disappeared.

So far as my first wife and my second wife and my divorce are concerned, I have given the essential facts quite plainly and I will not repeat them here. In both cases there was an intense mutual affection. And a dissatisfaction. I have never been able to discover whether my interest in sex is more than normal. There is no meter yet for that sort of thing. I am inclined to think that I have been less obsessed by these desires and imaginations than the average man. Occasional love reveries, acute storms of desire, are in the make-up of everyone. But in my case they have never dominated my scientific curiosities, my politico-social urge, or my sense of obligation. Yet they have never been suppressed; because my mental constitution is averse from suppression. It accepts "Thou shalt not" with extreme reluctance and a sustained protest. And my circumstances have been quite extraordinarily free. I have had no considerable restraints from the outside upon realizing my imaginations. I was not under such prohibitions as we impose upon lawyer, doctor or schoolmaster. Except in so far as affection put barriers about me, I have done what I pleased; so that every bit of sexual impulse in me has expressed itself. Most other men probably have as much or more drive, I suspect, but less outlet. Their sexual lives are forced to be more furtive than mine, and they are in consequence more subject to complexes. So long indeed as Jane and I were in a desperate and immediate struggle with the world, there was no scope for any wanderings of my desires, and we managed to carry on with the limited caresses and restricted intimacies her relative fragility and her relative lack of nervous and imaginative energy imposed upon us. But with success, an ampler life and more vigorous health, our close strict partnership was relaxed. I began to think of lovelier sensual experiences and to ask "Why not?" So far as literary expression goes, and as far as my relations to Jane go, I have dealt with this quite openly in my *Autobiography* in the sections called "*Modus Vivendi*" and "Writings about Sex." But not so far as other personalities are concerned. Here I want to set down, so far as I am able, the emotional phases and personal encounters that—evident to every penetrating reader—were going on concurrently with this revolt against the definite sexual code of the time.

To do that adequately I think I must begin by speculating a little about a certain factor I believe to be present in every normally constituted brain. I have been theorizing about my mental processes and perhaps later on I shall be able to release my conclusions in some speculative or artistic form; because I find them very interesting. But here I will just set them down as they occur to me. I think that in every human mind, possibly from an extremely early age, there exists a continually growing and continually more subtle complex of expectation and hope; an aggregation of lovely and exciting thoughts; conceptions of encounter and reaction picked up from observation, descriptions, drama; reveries of sensuous delights and ecstasies; reveries of understanding and reciprocity; which I will call the Lover-Shadow. I think it is primarily sexual and then social—I mean sexual in origin, because I do not see how a living creature could ever be anything but self-centred except through the development of sexual, family and group mental systems. I think it is almost as essential in our lives as our self consciousness. It is *other* consciousness. No human being faces the world in conscious complete solitude; no human being, I believe, lives or can live without this vague various protean but very real presence side by side with the *persona*, something which says or says in effect, "Right-O," or "Yes" or "I help" or "My dear." That is what I mean by the Lover-Shadow. It is the inseparable correlative to the *persona*, in the direction of our lives. It may be deprived of all recognition; it may be denied; but it is there. Even when a man sings

> "I care for nobody, no not I,
> And nobody cares for me,"

he sings to his Lover-Shadow. Or he would not sing.

And again when a drunken sailor ashore declares, "I wanna woman," it is, in the crudest form, his Lover-Shadow he is demanding. His need may be primarily physical, but his *persona* will have to be satisfied also if he is to be properly gratified. He'll talk to the bitch; he'll show off; he'll hear about her and sympathize.

Books, poems, pictures; it is for the Lover-Shadow they are written. A vast proportion of human conduct is explicable only as a continual urge in the mind to realize, more or less completely, something if not all of the Lover-Shadow, some aspect at least, some gleam of that complex of craving and hope. The normal disposition, especially in the adolescent and the young adult, is to concentrate most or all of the Lover-Shadow in the mate; sometimes the friend but more usually the lover. In the more complex mammals the concentration of the Lover-Shadow is considerable but perhaps never total. When we make love, we are trying to make another human being concentrate for us as an impersonation or at least a symbol of the Lover-Shadow in our minds; and when we are in love it means that we have found in someone the presentation or the promise of some, at least, of the main qualities of our Lover-Shadow. The beloved person is for a time identified with the dream—attains a vividness that captures the rôle, and seems to leave anything outside it unilluminated.

The greater, the more complex the Lover-Shadow we carry with us becomes when we are "head over heels in love," almost or altogether invisible in the background of our bright excitement, and only as the magic of that condition exhausts itself, do we realize that this ampler reciprocal to one's *persona* is still waiting there behind it all, a criticism, a qualification, an exacting standard.

(The *persona* and the Lover-Shadow are, as I see it, the hero and heroine of the individual drama most of us make of our lives, but I do not want to convey that they are the whole cast of the piece. Many other complex systems move across that stage and play their rôle; fear and aversion systems, for example; skill systems and special appetences. But they are subordinate, deflecting and not directing systems.)

The sustaining theme of my *Experiment in Autobiography* has been the development and consolidation of my *persona*, as a devotee, albeit consciously weak and insufficient, to the evocation of a Socialist World-State. If I have not traced the development of my Lover-Shadow, and my search for its realization in responsive flesh and blood, with the same particularity and continuity, I have at least given the broad outline of its essential beginnings. I have told how it was framed. Almost from its indeterminate onset, the quality of my Lover-Shadow became as unequivocally feminine as my *persona* was unequivocally male; the demarcation of my heterosexuality became absolute quite early. There perhaps my imagination was rather more male than is normal. The bodily symbolization in my reveries of the Lover-Shadow in feminine form was always a little on the brave and noble side, because, I suppose, of that lurking infantalism to which I owe the breadth and simplicity of my outlook on life. But there was no element of worship in the attitude of my *persona* towards the Lover-Shadow. With me the Lover-Shadow never became, as it becomes in many cases, a sought-after saint or divinity. My innate self conceit and the rapid envelopment and penetration of my egotism by socialistic and politically creative ideas was too powerful ever to admit the thought of subordinating my *persona* to the Lover-Shadow. This fair and lovely person, who was to be my protagonist, was to be friendly and understanding; she was to understand me and my warfare of ideas. I do not recall that in the opening and formative phases of my life I had any dream or thoughts of my finding something perplexing in her and studying to understand her. I did not tease myself about that. She was to be a lovely, wise and generous person wholly devoted to me. Her embraces were to be my sure fastness, my ultimate reassurance, the culmination of my realization of myself. I developed the feminine embodiment of the Lover-Shadow so early—I was acutely conscious of sex by the time I was nine or ten—that I never evolved any religious aspect of the Lover-Shadow. Before the divinity could develop personality or any effect of relationship, the idea of an earthly feminine lover had cut the ground from his feet. There again I think I was normal. I think those minds to which such a phrase as "Jesus, Lover of my Soul" or "Sun of my Soul, Thou Saviour dear" carry any quality of reality constitute a minority of the human population. They certainly exist, but they are outside the range of my experience or imaginative feeling.

This great Shadow, so largely feminine, stood over me,

beside that expansion of myself, my *persona*—which I was developing out of reverie, as a man of science, as a leader in human affairs—even while I walked, as I have described, on a Sunday fifty years ago, in my shabby top-hat, with Isabel in Regent's Park. This was the standard by which later I was to measure her and myself and our life together. That phantom dwarfed and dominated us. And the same dream of inaccessible understanding and reciprocating womanliness waited still in the background of my divorce and through the years of adjustment with Jane, while I was making those queer endless "picshuas" which turned the physical defects and compromises of my second married life into a fantasy of tolerable affectionate absurdity, and left the larger dream-world free for dreams.

With the Lover-Shadow there is no flaw upon the physical ecstasy of love. The whole body of human poetry insists upon that. In these matters, as in dream-fantasies, there is no sense of proportion. The cosmogony of Tintoretto's *Origin of the Milky Way* has never shocked the human imagination. I found my hungry search for some realization of my inachieved desire roving involuntarily among the girls and women of my widening acquaintance. Some of them, old Nature, whispering in my blood, was persuading me, might have it, *must* have it, in their power to give me at least a transitory ecstatic physical realization of my *persona* that I had not yet attained. The glamour of the Lover-Shadow, as it detached itself and stood aloof from the every-day intimacies in the foreground of my life, fell wide and far. I tell here of myself what is perhaps an almost universal story for men and women alike. "Every woman is at heart a rake," said Pope; and—to complete the statement—every man. With an immense variation in proportion and degree.

§2
The Lover-Shadow across Pimlico and Soho

I suppose my memory and my self protectiveness would conspire to play a score of tricks upon me if I tried to tell, with any precision, the subtle and elusive tentatives by which the incompatibility of my Lover-Shadow with the realities of my successive marriages was betrayed. I have told, in the *Autobiography*, of my cheerful flash of sensuality with Isabel's assistant, and I suppose, if I had not lost all trace of her in the disorganization of my divorce, that I should have drifted towards her again later. I was at first extremely disingenuous with myself about these wanderings of my imagination. Large parts of my mind wanted to sustain the conception of a complete and happy unison with Jane, and still more extensive was the desire to maintain a façade of complete and happy unison. And I liked my work and my success, and I did not want my reputation to be clouded or my work disordered. But I can remember moods and phases, as early as my Woking days, when I wandered upon a bicycle about the highways and byways of Surrey, indisposed to force romantic events, but extraordinarily desirous that something that had still to come out of the Lover-Shadow should happen to me. But nothing came out of these solitary rides except a book called *The Wheels of Chance*.

I have told in the *Autobiography* of my schoolfellow Sidney Bowkett and how we helped to educate each other. He vanished from my life and went to America before I went from Midhurst to London, and he reappeared when I was just becoming known as a writer, and while I was still in my first home at Woking. I saw his name in the paper as defendant in a case of plagiarism; Beerbohm Tree had made a success in London with a dramatization of Du Maurier's *Trilby*, and Bowkett seems to have been touring the provinces with an illicit version based on a shorthand note of the Tree play. His name, Sidney Pitt Bowkett, was unmistakable, and I wrote to him a sort of "Hello" letter.

He turned up at Woking as surprised to find that I was a rising novelist as I was to discover him a rather unorthodox playwright, and it entertained us extremely to find all sorts of rough parallelisms in our adventure with life. He had gone off to America in a small dramatic company and had become a sort of understudy to Ted Henley, the brother of my W.E. Henley. His youthful bright attractiveness had interested various experienced actresses in his career, and he had returned to Europe in very much the rôle that had taken him to America, but much more talkative, half actor (he was far too self-conscious ever to act well) and half theatrical hanger-on. He had fallen in love with a vividly pretty blue-eyed Jewess who was an art student; she was just Jane's age; they had eloped and married at St. Pancras Registry Office, while we had married in Marylebone, and he had settled down with her to write plays in a little cottage at Thames Ditton, while I had settled down to write books at Woking. But he had not settled down to work with any of the doggedness with which I had settled down. He had learnt to sniff cocaine in America (unsettlement is the actor's life); he was writing little and beginning to fall away from the good resolutions of his marriage towards a life of incoherent lunges and adventures that was to end at last in morphino-mania and insanity. I did not realize at the time that he was starting upon the career of a drug-taker. Chitterlow in *Kipps* is a sketch of him in his Thames Ditton phase.

For a time, until his intensifying monologue and a subtle mutual exasperation estranged us, we were much together. We both worked for irregular spells and then went off together upon bicycles for days or half-days among the Surrey and Sussex lanes, and there was a mutual understanding that he knew all that there was to be known about plays, while I, to balance it, was a little compendium of literary art. But like Frank Harris and Bland, the chief topic of Sidney Bowkett was Wonderfulness among Women. Now I have tried to show in my story how the Lover-Shadow had developed in my life, and that it was a very grave and lively complex of desire. This stream of rakish boasting flowed across that gathering drive and had, I realize now, a stronger effect upon it than I perceived at the time. It vulgarized it and made it practical. Inherently, I wanted to meet and love and be loved by the Lover-Shadow, but through suggestion and competitiveness, in a sort of response to the brag and implications of these associates, brag and implications reflected endlessly by the contemporary stage and novel, I wanted, for my own self-respect, to *get* women. The Lover-Shadow was, I began to feel, elusive dream-stuff. The reality of women was something which was glad and happy to be brag-material for such swaggering males as Bowkett, Harris and Bland. All through this "Postscript to *Experiment in Autobiography*" the sensitive reader will detect the strain of essential vulgarity about sex, coming out in quick response to these codpiece-minded males. I am disposed to blame them for a streak that was in me already. Even now I smirk if anyone suggests that I have been a gay lad in these matters.

So the very lively bent of my mind towards a Shelley-like liberalism of sexual conduct, which I have described in my *Autobiography*, was supplemented by the growth of this coarser, less fastidious disposition to *get* girls and women, and, as my freedom of movement increased and opportunity multiplied about me, I found myself first of all trying to get, and then getting them, on the slightest attraction, with an increasing confidence of method. I think it is straining the word "love" to call these *amours* "love affairs." In all my life I think I have really loved only three women steadfastly; my first wife, my second wife and Moura Budberg, of whom I will presently tell. I do not know if I loved Rebecca West, though I was certainly in love with her towards the latter part of our liaison. I had one great storm of intensely physical sexual passion and desire with Amber Reeves. Beyond that, all these women I have kissed, solicited, embraced and lived with, have never entered intimately and deeply into my emotional life. I have liked them, found them pretty, exciting, amusing, flattering to the secret rakish braggart in my composition. I was jealous of them as one is jealous in a partnership, and jealous about them as one is jealous in a competition—and my impression is that I got nothing better than I gave. I was loved as I loved. Once I raised a storm of crazy love-hatred that I found very repellent and pitiful, but for the rest the exchanges were fairly equal—two libertines met—and when I *got* a woman, a woman *got* a man.

Yet each affair, cool-hearted though it was, had its individuality. Some at least of these encounters had a loveliness, often a quite accidental loveliness. They could be like flower-shows or walks in springtime or mountain excursions. Few ended bitterly, and most left a residue of friendliness and understanding. I cannot make up my mind that I regret any of them. And yet, unreasonably and illogically, there spreads over all this system of memories a haze of regret. The fundamental love of my life is the Lover-Shadow, and always I have been catching a glimpse of her and losing her in these adventures.

The first wanderings of my desires are very hard to trace. I was disposed to covet Bowkett's wife; and when Dorothy Richardson came to Worcester Park she and I took a special grave interest in each other. (I am Hypo in her "Miriam" novels.) Such glimpses of errant desire occur in the life of every curate. It was only when Spade House was building, that I found myself trying definitely to *get* anyone.

My journalistic career had brought me into contact with E. F. Nisbet, the dramatic critic of *The Times*, a queer intelligent Scotsman whose imagination had led him into a string of furtive seductions. He confided in me to a certain extent. He had an illegitimate daughter at a school at Goudhurst, in Kent, and when presently he died suddenly, leaving nothing whatever to support this child, I undertook her school expenses, had her at Sandgate for her holidays, and did what I could to launch her in life as a music teacher. I took on these obligations before I had set eyes upon her—in a mood of sentimental regret for old Nisbet. Later on I paid for a year for her at the School of Dramatic Art.

May Nisbet appeared as a gawky and rather sullen girl of fifteen or sixteen, who developed in a year or so into a budding young woman. She was not an intellectually active being; I never got to any close understanding or friendliness with her; but one day upon the beach at Sandgate she came down towards me wearing a close-fitting bathing-dress; instantly she seemed the quintessence of sunlit youth to me, and I was overwhelmed by a rush of physical desire, and the imaginative excitement that is so closely associated with it.

I never gratified that physical desire, and the story of this relationship, as I remember it, is a mixture of attempts to fulfil my benevolent intentions towards her—and also, in some way not too mean and ugly, to get her and make her mine. But no way opened that was not too mean and ugly; she had no romantic imaginativeness to respond to and develop my advances; she had indeed nothing whatever for me, and the outcome of the affair was a book, *The Sea Lady*, in which I sublimated my perplexities. As a symptom *The Sea Lady* is an interesting book, because it shows how extensive was the domination of feminine beauty and sensuous beauty in my Lover-Shadow at that time.

I made love to May Nisbet, but quite vaguely and inconclusively; our minds had nothing in common; no common humour nor sympathy; and after a time there was a relaxation of the tension between us, and with a certain helpful friendliness, she was pushed out of my life. She became a music teacher and a not very successful actress; she married, and passed out of my world. Her husband was a German and the war separated them. She has taught music and kept a school. Occasionally I have helped her in various small ways; I have seen her quite recently and she has no more appeal for me now than any other human being. Yet long ago she quickened my imagination with the desire for a sunlit beautiful body. In some way that had to be assuaged.

In this phase of unrest, at some crowded gathering of writers, I met Violet Hunt, a young woman a little older than myself, who had already written and published several quite successful novels. She had a nervous lively wit laced with threads of French—for her mother was French. Her father was a Pre-Raphaelite painter. Her body still lives prettily in one or two of Boughton's paintings. We talked of social questions, literary work, and the discomforts and restlessness of spinsterhood. She had grown up in Pre-Raphaelite circles; she had been the mistress of an adventurer named Crawford; he had left her, and she was full just then of the same restless craving for the clasp of an appreciative body as myself.

So we came to an understanding, and among other things she taught me were the mysteries of Soho and Pimlico. We explored the world of convenient little restaurants with private rooms upstairs, and the struggling lodging-houses which are only too happy to let rooms permanently to intermittent occupants. So without any great disturbance of our literary work and our ostensible social lives, we lunched and dined together and found great satisfaction in each other's embraces. We concentrated the haunting Lover-Shadow into a thrill and so escaped for a time from our desire. And when presently the Lover-Shadow returned and demanded incarnation we exorcized it once more. So I was able to give the major part of my mental activities to the broader interests of my life.

There was little or no pretence of an exclusive preoccupation between Violet Hunt and myself. There were one or two other *passades* about this time of the same mutually accommodating type. Ella D'Arcy, who wrote one or two vivid short stories in the *Yellow Book*, had a kindliness for me, and the latent adventurousness between Dorothy Richardson and myself was consummated. Dorothy's precision and innate truthfulness have deserted her in her account of her love affair with "Hypo" in *Dawn's Left Hand*. She has forgotten a night and a day we spent between Eridge and Frant, and how we made love in the bracken. For me it was a sensuous affair, for Dorothy was then a glowing blonde. But, as her book shows, she wanted some complex intellectual relationship, and I have never been able to talk to Dorothy. She wanted me to explore her soul with wonder and delight. But a vein of evasive ego-centred mysticism in her has always made her mentally irritating to me; she seemed to promise the jolliest intimate friendship; she had an adorable dimple in her smile; she was most interestingly hairy on her body, with fine golden hairs, and then—she would begin intoning the dull clever things that filled that shapely, rather large, flaxen head of hers; she would lecture me on philology and the lingering vestiges of my Cockney accent, while there was not a stitch between us. The adventurous student who cares to turn up her *Dawn's Left Hand* may confirm these statements.

A woman from Australia wrote to me about *Kipps* and asked me to come and see her at her lodging. I visited her several times, and I remember her still for her ruddy sunburnt skin and straw-coloured hair.

Neither at this promiscuous phase of my life nor at any time did I have much intercourse with prostitutes. Always it has been necessary for me to have a friendly and personal element in my love-making, and to imagine that I am wanted as much as I want. Mostly my experience with *Venus Meretrix* has occurred in foreign places, when I have found myself alone and lonely—when indeed it was solitude rather than the Lover-Shadow that oppressed me—and all my memories of them are kindly. I like them as a class. There is a realism and an unpretending kindness about them that appeals to me. They must endure a lot from drunken, brutish and shame-faced men; they are receptacles for much boasting and posturing and patronage, and it is not difficult to be civil to them and take the humiliation out of their business for an hour or so.

In 1906, as I have told in my *Autobiography*, I went to America and talked to President Roosevelt the First. Our conversation was posed at a high level. After I left him that afternoon, I had a reaction. The air was warm and languorous, and I had nothing to do before dinner. I was faced by a frightful stretch of empty time, and at the time I did not want to think any more about my White House conversation. I called a cab and told the driver to take me to a "gay house." This was before the moral purgation of Washington. "White or Coon?" he said. It seemed to me that I ought to experience the local colour at its intensest. "Coon," said I.

I found myself standing drinks to a number of frizzy-haired brown women in exiguous costumes, in a sort of reception room. We talked politely about Washington in the summer, and whether the Washington Monument (still incomplete at that date) could ever be finished. The face of a slender bright-eyed woman attracted me. I went and sat beside her and presently I went to her room.

We talked, and our mutual liking increased. She was a mixture of white and Indian and negro, dark-haired and with a skin the colour of smooth sea sands, and, I thought, much more intelligent than most of the women one meets at dinner-parties. She was a reader of books, and she showed me some verse she had attempted; she had been learning Italian, because she wanted to go to Europe, see Europe, and come back "White" as a pseudo-Italian. Our love-making was done presently in an atmosphere of friendliness; we forgot our mercenary relation until it was time for me to go. "I'll hope to see you again," she said. "I like you." But I could make no promises, because I was leaving Washington next day. I said I would do what I could to come to her again. When it came to the parting present, I gave her a bill rather larger than was customary.

She glanced at it, and said in a flat voice, "But do you *mean* this?"

"Ah, then I know," she said, "I shall never see you again! I see, my dear. Never mind, but I see. Don't go yet for just a little while. I want you to stay with me for a little longer."

We who had not known of each other's existence at three o'clock parted like lovers at half-past six. We had become linked together by our mutual liking. And nothing could better illustrate how closely and far and swiftly tendrils of interest spread from bodily sensuality and imaginative excitation, out into the rest of the individuality. No sexual encounter leaves two people indifferent; they either hate or love. Neither of us knew the other's name, and she knew hardly anything whatever about me except that I was English, and yet the web wove about us so fast that it was hard not to make some foolhardy suggestion of co-operating in that European tour, or getting her at least to come to New York, or postponing my departure. Sanity prevailed with us, but for years I thought of her at times with tenderness, and it may be that at times she recalled a kindred regard for me.

We play with the sexual side of the Lover-Shadow; we relieve and drug the dissatisfaction of our imaginations in a purely sexual adventure, and suddenly sex turns upon us and grips us. We slip off to the little restaurant, the house of assignation; we creep up the staircase and along the corridor; we hide together in the thicket, and it is just to be a bright, almost momentary, flash of indulgence, and, before we know where we are, the haunting deeper need to possess and be possessed, for good and all, that undying hunger of the soul for a commanding love-response, has laid hold upon us.

When I think of all the areas of all the great cities, the restaurants, meeting places, sly rooms, the daily hundreds and thousands of thousands devoted to the restless dangerous unsatisfying search for temporary assuagement of the undying desire for the Lover-Shadow, I am half disposed to sympathize with Origen, and scream for peace and chastity at any price. For the thing has grown up with the development of the human mind to a vast distressful preoccupation. It will not leave us alone, and it will not give us enduring peace of mind. To make love periodically, with some grace and pride and freshness, seems to be, for most of us, a necessary condition to efficient working. It admits of no prosaic satisfactions. It is a mental and aesthetic quite as much as a physical need. I resent the necessity at times as much as I resent the perpetual recurrence of meal-times and sleep.

§3
Dusa

In the autobiography I have told how I tried to turn the Fabian Society into a sort of Communist Party, the Samurai of the *Modern Utopia*, and I have hinted at the infirmities of character and purpose that wrecked that attempt. The core of that failure was the inflammation of my sexual egotism by the peculiar conditions of excitement created by the struggle. It was logical to carry the appeal for devotion to the cause of socialism, for a closer liaison with Labour politics, and for an expansion of propaganda—to the young, to the sons and daughters of the socialists and liberals, and to the young insurgents who are to be found in every generation of university students. The Fabian meetings, which had been sober and decorous disputations, with only a slight flavouring of Hubert Bland, became suddenly very bright and animated gatherings of the young. The rumour of scenes and commotions drew in a contingent of those responsive schoolteachers, secretaries, students and so forth, young women of restricted life and limited social opportunity, who drift through every great city in search of entertainment and participations. An English "intelligentsia" suddenly appeared—as I recorded a little later, in *Ann Veronica*.

A number of these young women assumed attitudes of discipleship towards me. The earnest discussion of political issues with small groups of three or two, the formation of distinctive friendships, pedestrian duologues, ensued. Biography, and what one might call mutual character-caressing, crept into the social and political theme. It was inevitable that some of these instructive friendships should presently take a warmer tinge. Post-war laxity of sexual behaviour had still to come, and the breaking-down of barriers to love-making was an unformulated irregular process. In that hothouse atmosphere of the Bland household at Dymchurch and Well Hall, which I have already described in the *Autobiography*, I found myself almost assigned as the peculiar interest of Rosamund, the dark-eyed sturdy daughter of Bland and the governess, Miss Hoatson. Rosamund talked of love, and how her father's attentions to her were becoming unfatherly. I conceived a great disapproval of incest, and an urgent desire to put Rosamund beyond its reach in the most effective manner possible, by absorbing her myself. Miss Hoatson, whose experiences of life had made her very broad-minded, and who had a queer sort of liking for me, did not seem to think this would be altogether disastrous for her daughter; but presently Mrs. Bland, perceiving Hubert's gathering excitement in the tense atmosphere about us, precipitated accusations and confrontations. Bland stirred up her strain of anti-sexual feeling.

She wrote insulting letters to Jane, denouncing her tolerance of my misbehaviour—which came rather oddly from her. Rosamund was hastily snatched out of my reach and, in the resulting confusion, married to an ambitious follower of my party in the Fabian Society, Clifford Sharp—and so snatched also out of the range of Hubert's heavy craving for illicit relations. It was a steamy jungle episode, a phase of coveting and imitative desire, for I never found any great charm in Rosamund. I would rather I had not to tell of it. But in that damned atmosphere that hung about the Blands, everyone seemed impelled towards such complications; it was contagious, and I want the reader to understand these mental infections.

From this aberration on my part there began a little trickle of hints and whisperings, anonymous letters and so forth, with the conflicts for the reconstruction of the Fabian organization, and presently this swelled to an embarrassing spate by a second lapse in the same style.

The dangerous stuff I had been writing about the communal marriages of the Samurai, taken straight from Plato, had seized upon some of the more animated and imaginative of the girl students who had come crowding into the Fabian Society when my campaign woke it up. Some of them developed a zeal for its practical realization. Among them was Amber Reeves, the daughter of a man who had been very friendly towards me for some years. She fell in love with me with great vigour and determination, and stirred me to a storm of responsive passion.

The Reeves couple were in a complex tangle with each other. Pember Reeves had been a promising New Zealand politician with a strong socialistic disposition. He had a good, but unoriginal, mind, and he had patterned himself on the English university ruling-class type. He imagined a liberal, scholarly *persona* for himself. He liked to think himself as of good family and traditions. He was not an adventurous or acquisitive man, but he had a strong sense of proprietary right. He married in New Zealand an extremely pretty young woman, considerably younger than himself, with a streak of Hungarian blood. Like so many men of outward purity and unblemished reputation, he stamped upon her mind that the sexual side of marriage was a very nasty, painful and discomforting affair—with prompt consequences. There were two daughters and a son (who later was killed in the war). It is characteristic of Reeves that, when he started with his wife upon their honeymoon, he asked her if she had any money with her. "I'd better take care of that," he said, and thereafter for many years she was strictly allowanced and had to account for all her spending. He never allowed what were then the new ideas about birth control to come near her. She went through the secret dismay, the secret rebellion, the choice between open defiance and subtle evasions and deceptions, that must have been, and perhaps still is, the inner history of hundreds of thousands of respectably married young women. I don't think she ever dreamt of escape through a lover. That was entirely outside her philosophy—and opportunities. To begin that nasty business over again with another male rough!—she would as soon have escaped through a sewer. And Pember Reeves was wide awake to guard his pretty misused treasure from the advances of bad men.

He found his way to high political success in New Zealand barred by the hostility of Seddon. It was a convenient way of clearing out a formidable rival from the colonial field to send him to London as Agent-General and—with the warm approval of his wife—Pember Reeves came to London. He was not so much accepting defeat as expanding his ambition, for already there had been an instance in Bob Lowe and there was presently to be another in Bonar Law, of a man with a colonial training making a brilliant English political career. But Pember Reeves had not the vigour of initiative needed for distinction in the London world. He cultivated a number of friends; for the Webbs, for example, he figured as a respectable Liberal with Leftward tendencies; he was a member of that talking club, the Coefficients, I have described in the *Autobiography*, and he remained Agent-General for New Zealand—"High Commissioner" it became later. People found his wife charming, but he still kept her under restraint, so to speak; his conversation was informative and argumentative rather than flexible and entertaining, and he achieved no sort of social success.

I met him first at a Royal Society dinner whither I had gone as the guest of Ray Lankester, and he picked upon me to be very friendly. He was writing an essay upon "Utopias, Ancient and Modern." He got me to come into the Savile Club; he came down to stay at Spade House with Henry Newbolt, and presently the two families were exchanging hospitalities very freely and frequently. I never got to any very close intimacy with him; he knew nothing of himself, he saw the world classically, his best talk consisted of estimates of immediate political persons and possibilities; but both Jane and I discovered his wife to be a very subtle and interesting person. She was then about forty; still full of humour, a very bright talker, and working out a sort of liberation for herself from the matrimonial flattening she had undergone. She liked me, and she liked very much to talk to me, and she talked very intimately of many things in life that she found perplexing.

She had worked out a curious sublimation of her secret rebellion against her husband; she had become, almost before he realized what was happening, a leading suffragette. The same way of escape was found by the wife of another tyrannous husband, Mrs. W.W. Jacobs, and I made a book out of that type of reaction that I think may survive as a fragment of social history, *The Wife of Sir Isaac Harman*. She began speaking at a drawing-room meeting or so; it seemed harmless enough, and then she launched out gravely and resolutely into journeys about the country to meetings here and conferences there. Any other gadding about he would have suppressed, but the blessed "Movement" had his formal approval. She would vanish from the house for days upon some distant mission; on the staircase she would meet the weary Titan coming home from the toils of imperial statecraft, and she would be dressed to go out to dinner by herself. "I told you about it weeks ago." She had now a certain amount of money of her own; some aunts had died, and this time she had avoided handing the bequests over to him for safe-keeping. Seizing upon his association with the Fabians, she also came into the Committee of the Fabian Society. She stuck most loyally to me through all my clumsy and unsuccessful efforts to broaden the conception of socialism to include sexual emancipation, and expand the Labour Fabian movement into a propaganda for a new way of human living.

A side of their lives that then was kept turned away from my criticism was their propensity, which hardened later into a belief, to take Christian Science seriously. They felt, I think, that I might deal with it destructively; and in some subtle way, with each of them, repudiation of physical ill-health and medical authority attracted them. It liberated something in them both to ascribe their feelings of malaise and their phases of illness and dullness to some failure of faith and will in themselves. I think she was the first to be drawn to this crude materialistic mysticism, and she came to it in close relation to her insurgent feminism. She hated the admission of inferiority implied by the periodic disablement of women, and she denied its physical reality. So she made her growing daughters go cycling or walking in the rain when they ought to have been resting at home, and she fought incipient colds with draughts in an ultra-British fashion. I never knew a household so firmly convinced that windows were made to be opened.

Reeves had a badly adjusted nervous system, by nature, I think; there may have been some clash in his heredity; he had fits of indigestion very easily, bad head-aches and phases of insomnia, and as he lost his early overbearing energy, and his wife acquired skill and resolution in the conflict of their wills, he found his hypochondria countered by a bracing treatment and by appeals to him to assert his essential healthiness. No doctor was ever consulted for the pains and lassitudes and bad moods that increased in his life. As far as possible he ignored them, and clung to his conception of his *persona* as a transplanted English gentleman of culture, who had had a whiff of the "great open spaces" in his New Zealand home, had done his appointed work there, and returned to the Old Country to play his part in liberal progress.

Following the best traditions of English liberalism, he interested himself in South-Eastern Europe, and "championed" Greeks as Trevelyans championed Italians and Buxtons Bulgarians. He discoursed without let or hindrance in his home on Eastern European politics, his New Zealand land reform and similar topics. His wife and family never argued with him or broached topics that might irritate him. They led their own lives round and about him; they circumvented him. Their gathering indifference to his comfort and routines at home—based on the Christian Science antagonism to indulgence—made him a frequent figure at the Savile and Reform Clubs.

The Pember Reeves family was, in fact, already in a phase of dissociation when I came to know it first in 1904.

Presently, the eldest daughter, Amber, came into our group. She was then a girl of brilliant and precocious promise. She had a sharp, bright, Levantine face under a shock of very fine abundant black hair, a slender nimble body very much alive, and a quick greedy mind. She became my adherent and a great propagandist of Wellsism at Newnham College.

Her mother encouraged the development of a very intimate friendship between us. It did not seem possible to her that any harm could possibly arise from our constant association. Her mind was engaged in repudiating some of the most urgent facts in the human make-up. Just as she would hear nothing of fatigue or indigestion or intermittent illness, so she was doing her best to dismiss all love, romance, and, above all, desire, as a kind of unaccountable silliness that could not affect the kind of people one really knew and lived with. They were phantoms of the imagination, and you abolish them by never giving them a thought. She was trying to carry on her own bright life, make her speeches, attend her committees, meet people socially, in the clear definite world these negations left her. Her methods of getting away from Pember Reeves, by all sorts of little contrivances and frauds, were adopted by her daughter, and he was master in his own house of a family that systematically eluded him. Amber could vanish from the lunch-table or dinner-table, vanish on a visit to unknown friends, join unverifiable reading-parties, with a quite remarkable facility.

For a time I maintained our relationship of a great and edifying friendship at an austere level. We went for walks discussing social philosophy and suchlike questions with a considerable earnestness and sincerity. Amber was working in the Moral Science Tripos (she took Firsts in both Parts I and II) and I was trying to get my ideas in order in the various papers that developed into *First and Last Things*. Some of my suggestions cropped up in her examination papers and mingled with her own originality, and the systematic training in precision she was getting from her own university teachers, and especially from Dr. Ellis M'Taggart, made her a valuable astringent influence upon my phrasing.

But of necessity our talks grew more and more intimate, and she conceived the pretty fancy of calling me by the flattering name of "Master," while I was entrusted with her own special name of "Dusa." (This was short for Medusa, because in her schooldays she had a trick of imitating Cellini's *Medusa* head.) One day she broke the thin ice over my suppressions by telling me she was in love, and when I asked "with whom?" throwing herself into my by no means unwilling arms. The conception of group marriage and mutual solace, as I had embodied it in *A Modern Utopia*, provided all that was necessary for a swift mutual understanding, and we set about the business of making love with the greatest energy. We lay together naked in bed as a sort of betrothal that night; we contrived a meeting in Soho, when we became lovers in the fullest sense of the word, and before she went back to Cambridge for her examination for Part II of the Tripos, she went off, ostensibly to read by herself in an imaginary cottage of an imaginary friend in Epping Forest, but actually to join me in a lodging in Southend. There we had some days of insatiable mutual appreciation, which did not in the least impair her success with the Mental and Moral Science examiners. I remember lying on the beach with her and planning the thesis she was to write when she came to London. For her Cambridge career was to be prolonged as research student at the London School of Economics. And I remember also that, after our luggage had gone down to the waiting cab, we hesitated on the landing, lifted our eyebrows, and went back gleefully for a last cheerful encounter in the room we were leaving.

So soon as she was back in London, I took a room near Eccleston Square, and there we would go for a long day or a night or so, every eight or ten days. We would have long walks in London, dine at a restaurant, or she would buy a cold fowl and salad, and we would eat cheerfully like two buff savages in our room. And in the course of long walks, when we found ourselves strolling together in the country, there would be opportunity for embraces; it seemed very fresh and keen to make love among bushes in a windy twilight near Hythe, and a great lark to get a heavy key from the sexton to inspect the belfry of—was it Paddlesworth?—Church, and embrace in the room below the bells. And again in the woods on the way home. We liked to feel the faint flavour of sinfulness that current standards threw over us, and my memory of all these experiences glows still with unregretted exhilaration and happiness.

Now the theory of our relationship was that these excursions into sensuousness were the secret link that was to bind us in some very ambitious constructive work. All this time my own output was unimpaired, and I wrote as vigorously as ever I did, and swept aside a number of irrelevant distractions, because I knew that in a few days I could be clutching Amber's fuzz of soft black hair. And she too was supposed to be working strenuously. As I tell in my *Autobiography*, I had never been satisfied with the Socialist, and particularly with the Communist, theory of social motives, and I wanted her, for her London thesis, to attempt a more objective classification of motives and hindrances to social service, as they are found in different parts of the social structure. I wanted her to enquire, "Why and How are Men Citizens?" I think still that that might have been a very important piece of work. But it was never carried out.

It was never carried out because, firstly, Amber was mentally still too much of a pupil, too much in the student phase mentally, to grasp it and carry it out, and also because presently our liaison exploded into an outrageous scandal, and we were forced apart. So far as her own limitations are concerned, she had always been the swift responsive learner; she had a yielding mind and not an aggressive one; she had none of such obduracies and resistances in her as I had developed so freely under Professors Guthrie and Judd; and so soon as there was no longer any course of lectures to follow, any prescribed books to read, anything there to abstract and summarize, she was at a loss. She was entirely untrained for the enterprise of going into the thickets of fact with an interrogative hatchet and hewing out the frame of an answer. I have seen this happen to many successful students; travelling on beaten roads and blazed tracks is no training for the wilderness; and, in addition, Professor Hobhouse, to whom she took her first suggestions for approval, did not catch on to the general idea. She became discouraged; she slackened and lost steering way; she did not get on with the job. This left her exciting love-adventure unbalanced and tremendous in her mind; she found herself with time on her hands and unsettled; and, while I was keeping our secret close and tight, she gave way to a desire to talk about it and elaborate it. She was intensely proud of what she had done. She was overflowing with erotic adventurousness and pride.

She told some of the Newnham dons; she told her mother who, dismayed but valiant, did her best to take an enlightened view of the situation; she confided in her undergraduate friends. We found ourselves in conflict with a variety of standards. People protested and argued—in undertones, furtively—and for a time we went our way, unhindered. There is a good rendering of the ideals and imaginations of our situation in *The Research Magnificent*. But one aspect of the case I was not facing. I was theorizing about free love, but I was keeping Amber for myself. I was trying to maintain a triangular grouping. Jane was invincibly the wife, and Amber the young mistress; we all understood each other, we asserted, beautifully.

Meanwhile a trickle of whispered talk was undermining our unstable grouping, and Amber's unconcentrated mind was being attacked by a miscellany of divergent suggestions. A wave of philo-progenitiveness was passing through the intelligentsia, and she began to want a child by me, and to live with me more closely and continuously. This did not at all suit my obsession to "get on with the work," and my disposition to treat love as an incidental refreshment in life. I would not see that the linking force between us was the entirely normal relationship of male and female; and I was hanging on, long after Amber had slipped her hold upon it, to a dream of mental friendship and a close co-operation in politico-social effort.

It is easy now, at a distance of a quarter-century, to see the impossibility of this unstable situation we had made for ourselves. But at the time I was close up against it; it was happening to me just as much to everyone else concerned; I was not in control of it. If I had had a clearer vision of it, I think I should have set about—as Bolshevized Russians say—to "liquidate" the tangle. As the older, and so more responsible, lover, I ought, since I could not leave Jane to marry her, to have helped Amber to release herself from me. I ought to have realized that the splendid friendship had failed. I ought to have learnt my lesson then and there and taken defeat decently. It was not in me to do that, for the very simple reason that the erotic passion she had aroused in me was intense and would tolerate no separation. It had become a jealous fixation. I could not think of other women, or endure the thought of relinquishing her to any other man.

In the gaps between our times together, Amber was restless and active. She talked abundantly, and she had a following of animated friends. If she did not flirt with the young men, her contemporaries, she made herself very interesting and companionable to them. One or two wanted to marry her. With one of them in particular, G. R. Blanco White (who had been Second Wrangler and was now a barrister) she spent a good deal of her time. They would go off together on Sundays for long walks in the country. She told him of her intimacies with me and distressed him very much. He was a clear-headed, conscientiously consistent young man, and he saw the position and what it behoved me to do more plainly than I did. Unfortunately he set about forcing me to do it—in a vein of intense rivalry. She forced comparison upon him. He determined to rescue Amber from herself at any cost—for himself.

Hitherto Pember Reeves had gone his way, through all this net of intrigue, in a state of complete obliviousness. The anonymous letter-writer in the Fabian Society had wind of how matters stood, but she confined her attentions to Mrs. Reeves. But threats of exposure came to Amber, and the smouldering resentments of Bland awakened to ingenious subterranean activities. Now suddenly, with my will torn between all that Jane and my work meant for me and my chronic desire for the embraces of my mistress, I was confronted by the fact that everything was "coming out." I do not think for a moment that Amber imagined clearly that she would force my hand and oblige me to go through a divorce and marry her, but I do not see how that idea could have been absent from her mind. I think she too had her will dispersed in opposite directions. I was a great thing in her imagination and she did not want to injure me. But her life had now no unity; she was doing nothing at the London School of Economics, and default of all her brilliant promise—and she had been one of the brightest intellectual hopes of Feminism—hung over her at the end of the year. She could not have been reluctant to see matters hurrying to a crisis. Blanco White exploded the situation by going to Pember Reeves, explaining that I had "ruined" her, and offering to marry her. Pember Reeves became all that an eighteenth-century father should be. He made the whole affair a public scandal; he declared his intention of shooting me, and "saw red" with zealous thoroughness. Poor Mrs. Reeves was overwhelmed by shouts and accusations. The one thing necessary for her was to conceal from Reeves the fact of her tacit acquiescence through so many months in our liaison. She had a revulsion to accepted standards. Amber was to marry Blanco White now whether she liked it or no, and be damned grateful to him.

I am doing my best not to exculpate myself in this affair but to tell how things arose and what we all did. I was, by twists and turns, two entirely different people; the man for whom Jane's security and pride and our children and my work were the most precious things in life, and the man for whom Amber had become the most maddeningly necessary thing in life. Sometimes one of these men ruled me and sometimes the other. Amber was perhaps divided as widely between her desire for a passionate isolation with me and a quite natural wish for social rehabilitation, a life of coming and going with all her friends about her. She understood the forces that tore me, and she knew she could not trust me except to make an outcast heroic life for her that would have been intolerably hard to live.

When the sexual obsession was uppermost in me, all my theorizing about the open-living Samurai was flung to the winds. I wanted to monopolize her. And I do not know to this day how far that monopolization ever attracted her. But no doubt, other things being equal, she was quite prepared to monopolize me.

There was no logical development in our conduct, but only jagged masses of inconsistent impulse. I tell of the things we did, but I cannot answer the question: "Why did you do this thing?" With the storm gathering over us, Amber got through to me by telephone, and we went to our room near Victoria for the last time. "Give me a child," said Amber, "whatever happens," and that seemed heroic to me. I made no attempt to question this sudden philo-progenitiveness in her, and we set about the business there and then. She told Blanco White, but he persisted in his resolve to separate us and marry her. She packed a couple of valises and slipped off to meet me at Victoria Station. I carried her off to Le Touquet in France and took a little furnished chalet there. We looked isolation in the face.

We walked and talked about the silvery dunes, and sat and made love in the warm night darkness under the silent sweeping beams of the two lighthouses and discussed what lay before us. And having discharged all the force of sexual romanticism, the big chunks of motive that were detached from that complex altogether loomed immensely over us. Neither of us really wanted to carry out an elopement on nineteenth-century lines. I found the idea of a divorce from Jane intolerable. Neither of us relished the prospect of wandering about the Continent, a pair of ambiguous outcasts—quite possibly hard up. We wanted to have London and all its activities. I was for London and social defiance, but that was easier for me than Amber—because her mother had turned against her and she had no standing of her own. And that sort of thing is far easier now than it was before the war. Amber drooped. "I shall go back and marry Rivers." I took her to Boulogne, saw her aboard the boat, and returned to the chalet at Le Touquet.

I stayed there some days, unable to go back at once to the lustless decency of Sandgate and work. Then I sent for Jane to come over to me with the boys, and I did my best to entertain them. I forget exactly how I felt about it all then, but I think there was much wisdom in that step. With those cheerful youngsters about, I could go for walks, race, bathe, and get back across the gap of feeling that had opened between Jane and myself. When my mental confusion became too disagreeable, I would go off alone for a twelve-mile walk in new, and so in refreshing country. And I set to work upon what I think is one of my good books, *The History of Mr. Polly*. I think Mr. Polly's marriage-feast is not a bad piece of work, and it is odd to recall that some of the best of that I wrote weeping bitterly like a frustrated child. Jane was wonderful. She betrayed no resentment, no protesting egotism. She had never seen or felt our relationship as being primarily sexual or depending upon sexual preference. She had always regarded my sexual imaginativeness as a sort of constitutional disease; she stood by me patiently, unobtrusively waiting for the fever to subside. Perhaps if she had not been immune to such fevers I should not have gone astray. Presently we were talking about my case as though it was someone else in whom we were both concerned.

We decided to get out of Sandgate and the all too healthy, all too unstimulating life we led there. We had to escape from recurrent flat afternoons and evenings without an event. We would sell the house and go to a new home in London. I should see more people and vary my personal excitements. She had been starved for music, and there she could go to concerts— and the picture- and other art-shows that attracted her. We should both be taken out of ourselves. I should escape from the torments of physical jealousy in an unobtrusive promiscuity.

But that was not the end of things between myself and Amber. She married Blanco White and then had an immense recoil. She put it to me—ruthlessly. It is altogether unjustifiable, but that is what occurred. There was much vehement coming and going, and I made a complicated fluctuating fool of myself. It was her idea that Blanco White should not touch her until the child was born, and that she should be free to see me. I will not detail here the movements that ensued upon this, the tensions and exasperations of everyone concerned. None of the people involved, except for Jane and Blanco White, showed any singleness of purpose, and Amber least of all.

Both she and I clung most desperately to the idea that we were sustaining some high and novel standard against an obtuse and ignoble world. As a matter of fact, we had lost our flag long ago, when we allowed our liaison to be interrupted. We ought to have gone on meeting as lovers and saying "You be damned" to the world. If we had been separated for a time, we ought to have held out for our freedom and mutual preference. Then we should have done something. The child was an extraordinary irrelevance. It seemed a fine idea that afternoon, but it was destined to be the seed of a thin trickle of perplexing afterthoughts. Even in this jigsaw of explanation you can see that it doesn't quite fit.

The fiasco of our transitory elopement to Le Touquet was a development of that false situation. Thereafter we had no case. We ought to have thrown up the sponge and taken our punishment. Voluminous explanations flowed from me—and the more voluminous an explanation is, the less it explains. A pallid reflection of some aspects of our situation—or rather of the sentiments of our situation—appeared in *Ann Veronica* and *The New Machiavelli*. This was the underlying reason for the campaign against those books, which I have already described in the *Autobiography*. There were some weeks of a *ménage à trois* in a house I took from Elizabeth Robins in the Caterham Valley; there were intimate meetings elsewhere, and, up to the very birth of her daughter, I would call for Amber at her nursing-home in Cambridge Terrace, and take her gravely and publicly for walks in Hyde Park.

And still for a time after that event occasionally Amber and I would contrive to meet. But our flags were down and our pride had gone.

For some years about the war time we saw nothing of each other. Then we began to see each other again. She and her husband came and lunched with Jane and myself at Easton Glebe one Sunday. After Jane died, our meetings became more frequent; she and Blanco White came to dinner once or twice, and we resumed an open friendship. This would probably have happened earlier and more frankly, but for the risk of Pember Reeves hearing of it and making an uproar. Such an uproar would have hurt Jane while she was alive. But when she was dead I did not care a rap for any possible uproar. But I do not see much of Blanco White because I find him sententious and argumentative in an unimaginative way. I prefer, now that the conventions are satisfied, to entertain her alone. I take her to a theatre or the opera at times or we dine at a restaurant; we have collaborated in one of my books, and her daughter, the child of our crisis, regards me now as her real father, and she and her husband see me frequently. There is no passion and no jealousy between Amber and myself any more, but a very great intimacy and confidence. I think she feels she can count on my helpfulness in any sudden emergency—and I suppose I could count on her.

When Jane and I sold Spade House, we came to a pretty, decaying seventeenth-century house in Church Row, Hampstead, and presently—for purposes of work, and nervous relief—I took a minute flat in Candover Street off Great Portland Street. There I had a desk and wrote, and there I was visited by various friendly women from among that multitude of detached and discursive people who move through and on the margins of the world of intellectual activity. There Dusa came—among the others—and I found the bitterness of my loss of her was abating. I think that final sprinkling of adultery was a releasing thing for both of us. I was diffusing my imagination again and quieting down from our intensities.

And all the while I was working well, producing novels and short stories. *Mr. Polly* and *The New Machiavelli* belong to this period. But there is nothing of Dusa in these books. I had to get things in retrospect before I could do anything really like her. There is something of her early initiative in *Ann Veronica*. But in Amanda in *The Research Magnificent* (1915), Dusa, ever and again, comes through—at her most unscrupulous. And I tell there more of her than I do here, and much more than the like of ever happened; I develop her into a type, I guess with vision, rather too ruthlessly, and in the chapter called "The Assize of Jealousy," I display my own mental disposition and difficulties about these matters pretty completely. Lady Marayne also in that book is drawn from someone I knew very closely—as I will tell in the next section.

Yet I find I hesitate to begin that next section. Something has escaped me here. I have given Dusa in her adventurousness and her sensuality, and I have hinted at her lurking rascality. But there is a streak of stout friendliness in her mind and a courage in facing realities, even humiliating realities, that I have not got into the picture. Her mind had a training. Jane too had had a training. With the exception of Marjorie Craig, my daughter-in-law, who is also my secretary, I have never come close to any other feminine brains that had that trained disposition to veracity, even when it was a matter of disagreeable or humiliating realization. If any one of that three told a lie, she knew what she was doing. Dusa lied—but like a trickster and not essentially. Most women lie inwardly as well as outwardly. Women, as a rule, live in a mythical world even more than men do. They seek to evoke a personality and put it over us. They cannot go on living when that personality is denied. But the core of the love Amber gave me survived all the interpretations and exaltations of love-making. It has lived, and a certain love I bear her too has lived, in spite of our complete social detachment and the infrequency with which we met for many years. We have thought each other over and we find something good enough to keep in our memories. There is a natural affectionate understanding that is tacitly evident when we meet.

And Amber was not only instinctively but also intelligently and conscientiously a good mother. She brought up all her three children in a valiant poverty, a relative poverty, to be good workers with high standards, and when in succession she found her two daughters perplexing—both very modern and self-reliant young women, frankly taking lines of their own—she came to me to consider what was to be done about it. Blanco White was scrupulous and I was unscrupulous—and understood these things. It did not strike Amber as at all odd that she should consult me about Blanco White's daughter as well as our own.

In 1930 our daughter had become a first-class honours B.Sc. and a promising light of the London School of Economics. She was told the real story of her parentage and came to see me to be talked to properly. She knew my work and she found the idea of a blood link between us romantic and attractive. I found her a very clean-spirited keen-working reasonably ambitious young woman. But I will not wander beyond my proper autobiography. I do not think that a daughter can ever become fully a daughter if you have seen nothing of her from babyhood to maturity, but mine is a very dear friendly niece, so to speak, and we dine out and go to theatres together and are very pleasant to each other whenever she is in London.

And here, by way of a postscript, is an extract from a letter that came to me on August 25th, 1939. It pleases me very greatly that so our relationship should shape itself in Amber's thoughts.

> "We got back last night from Wales to find your book—it will be something to occupy our thoughts—a godsend. At a time like this, when life as we have known it seems to be ending for all of us, one's thoughts go back, and even if there were not the book to thank you for I think I should have written to thank you. What you gave me all those years ago—a love that seemed perfect to me, the influence of your mind, and our daughter—have stood by me ever since. I have never for a moment felt that they were not worth the price."

§4
The Episode of Little E

Among those kindly ladies who honoured me at Candover Street in the days before the war, helping me to get the fever for Amber out of my blood, there presently came one who decreed the end of that establishment. This was a very bright and original little lady indeed, the Gräfin von Arnim, the author of *Elizabeth and her German Garden.* She was Irish, with an Irish passion for absurdity and laughter, insincerely sentimental, and with an outlook upon life in which titles and social success were important. She was incapable of philosophical thought or political ideas. And withal she was a very shrewd, wise and witty little woman. She mingled adventurousness with extreme conventionality in a very piquant manner and I attracted her. She had eloped with von Arnim to Pomerania against the wishes of her family—her brother, Dr. Beauchamp, was a well-known Dublin physician—she had achieved a remarkable success with her first book, which she wrote in Pomerania to while away the tedium of her first pregnancy, and when, after several books plus babies, she found that von Arnim contemplated inflicting an endless tale of offspring upon her, she left him. She was intensely ignorant of all our modern lore of birth control, and altogether he gave her five children before their final break.

She could afford to leave him and come to England because the royalties from her early books made her much better off than he was. When she became my mistress he was already dead and she was a widow, still blackish in her costume, with a pretty house she had built in Switzerland between Sierre and Montana. She had found love-making with von Arnim a serious and disagreeable business, but she was aware that it might be far less onerous and more agreeable. She had already called upon us at Sandgate when she had been passing through Folkestone and had liked me; she heard talk of my scandalous life, and it seemed to her that I was eminently fitted to correct a certain deficiency in her own. I happened to go alone to lodge at a certain Cotchet Farm near Haslemere to complete some work, and she was staying with her sister Mrs. Waterlow about a couple of miles downhill towards Liphook. I forget now how far this proximity was arranged. We went for walks together over the heathery hillside, conversing upon life very cheerfully, and came to an easy understanding.

We liked each other; we laughed together; we made love very brightly, but I cannot imagine a relationship more free from passion than ours. Its practical convenience was undeniable. Jane had always felt a great admiration for the "Elizabeth" books and had not the slightest antipathy to our intimacy. She remarked that "Little e" could "make even German sound pretty." After the sunlight and moonlight of Cotchet Farm, Little e became the sole visitant at Candover Street. Presently Jane and I left our Church Row house and started a flat in St. James's Court and took Easton Glebe from Lady Warwick as a week-end house. Elizabeth too had a flat in St. James's Court. We carried on the liaison with an impudent impunity. We flitted off abroad and had amusing times in Amsterdam, Bruges, Ypres, Arras, Paris, Locarno, Orta, Florence—and no one was a bit the wiser. I stayed with her at her Chalet Soleil at Montana. It was in her humour to arrange, when that house was building, that the visitor's room in which I stayed should have a secret door behind a wardrobe which always moved on well-oiled castors. We said "Good night" in the passage to each other and whatever guests were with us and there was no subsequent creaking in the passage or any opening or shutting of doors. This lapse into nocturnal decorum was of profound importance to Little e because it seemed to her to give an absolute reassurance to any suspicions engendered by our day-time behaviour. When we were alone together, we would work hard in the mornings and prowl the mountain slopes in the afternoons, and make love perhaps on sun-flecked heaps of pine-needles under the straight trees. Generally we took a lunch with us of bread and ham in slices and beer and fruit. The peasants went about their business upon determinate lines; we knew where they were and where they were not, and except for them we never met a soul.

One day we found in a copy of *The Times* we had brought with us, a letter from Mrs. Humphrey Ward denouncing the moral tone of the younger generation, apropos of a rising young writer, Rebecca West, and, having read it aloud, we decided we had to do something about it. So we stripped ourselves under the trees as though there was no one in the world but ourselves, and made love all over Mrs. Humphrey Ward. And when we had dressed again we lit a match and burnt her. *The Times* flared indignantly and subsided and wriggled burning and went black and brittle and broke into fragments that flew away.

And we did many things like that. We went on walking tours with Teppy, her German companion, and stopped at various little chalet-inns. Twice we broke a bed—not very strong beds they were but still we broke them—and it was a cheerful thing to hear Little e—I doubt if she weighed six stone—explaining in pretty but perfect German why her bed had gone to pieces under her in the night.

Now this gay and innocent liaison might have lasted a long time and kept us both out of further trouble, but it came to an end because perhaps of the same freakish quality that had begun it. She had a teasing disposition and liked to vex me by sudden inconvenient changes of plan and by attacking things that might move me to anger. She wanted to get more out of me than the fun and fellowship I gave her. She wanted us to feel the keen edge of life together—in spite of the fact that we had both resolved it should never cut us. She developed a queer hostility to Jane. She hated the daily letters I wrote home to England and was jealous to see that the answers often amused and pleased me. More and more did she resent the fact that I kept our love light-hearted. She began to demand depth of feeling. Had I ever wept about her or trembled to come near her? *Real* lovers did. Would I ruin myself for her? Would I even interrupt my work for her? "Not a bit of it," I said, "for you or anyone." She began to scold me; she would sit up on the mountain turf in the sunlight scolding me and telling me the Whole Duty of a Lover, as she now conceived it. Then she began inventing nicknames for Jane; parodying Jane's way of talking; devising preposterous fantasies about her. She was comic and malicious and unendurable.

"This wasn't in the treaty," said I.

"This wasn't in the treaty," she mocked.

She was taking the fun out of our relationship and it was the fun that held us together.

Suddenly we stopped saying anything more about Jane; we began to talk with great politeness to each other about indifferent topics; Teppy was manifestly puzzled by the abrupt evaporation of badinage, and the wardrobe on its castors was undisturbed at night. I suppose each of us lay awake for hours expecting the other to come through in a state of surrender.

Then I said it was time for me to go back to England, and we parted with a sort of cordiality—but with no date fixed for another meeting. She was to return to St. James's Court in a few weeks' time.

We severed ourselves in a talk in her London drawing-room.

"It was your fault," she said. "You were only half a lover."

"It was your fault," I said. "You didn't really love."

"You don't know how much I have loved you."

"I think I do."

"You have been unfaithful to me since you came back to London."

"Does that matter—since we are parting?"

"Only half a lover," she sang. "Only half a lover."

There was no disputing it.

We did not meet again for some years. That was late in 1913. Her imagination turned to Earl Russell, who at that time had a house, Telegraph House, above Harting just close to Up Park, where my mother was once housekeeper. We had visited the Russells in the beginning of our affair, and I had felt my way along the passage to her room in the dark. There was a re-entrant angle that puzzled me extremely in the blackness, and the current Countess had a habit of sleeping with her door across the landing wide open. Little e even then found Russell an attractive misunderstood man who needed only an able wife to be reinstated socially. The current Countess was not a social success.

I do not know how far things went between Russell and Little e before the war, but the catastrophe of August 1914 made it highly desirable that she should recover British nationality. She got back from Switzerland to England with difficulty—a legal German. The Russells arranged a divorce and she became the new Countess Russell.

This saved her belongings in England from confiscation as alien property, but otherwise it was not a successful marriage. His temperamental defects and eccentricities are displayed with the most entertaining malice in her novel *Vera*. I do not think she would have written this book if he had not provoked her by writing and circulating a rather clumsy parody of an anonymous sentimental book of hers, *In the Mountains*. The description of his freaks of temper and tyranny and his house are absurdly true. But she inserted into her account of the hall of Telegraph House enlarged photographs of various members of the Russell family. This was too much for him. He met me in the Reform Club one day. "You know that wife of mine," he said, "and you know Telegraph House. You have read this book *Vera?* Now *is* it true that there are enlarged photographs of my relations in it?"

"It isn't," I said. "But she makes it highly probable. And after all *Vera* is a novel.... *Is* it meant for you, Russell?"

"Ugh," said Russell, realizing her hook in his gills.

I talked of something else.

She left him, but she would not divorce him, and he died still married to her. I met her again at a lunch-party in York Terrace; I forget completely now who was the hostess; we walked away together and found ourselves very good friends. She told me of Russell's iniquities. They blotted out my own completely. We have been good friends ever since, without a trace of malice between us.

She built a house in France, a few miles away from my own Lou Pidou, which I shall describe later, and we lunched and dined and gossiped together, so far as the bonds of jealousy and suspicion that held me at Lou Pidou permitted. We had always liked each other's humour and, now that there was no pretence of romantic love or urgent desire to distort our behaviour, we could laugh freely. Her malice against Jane had vanished and left no trace.

In February 1935 I visited her with Moura Budberg, and we had a very pleasant time together, and I made a dinner-party for her at the Sporting Club in Monte Carlo, which she enjoyed extremely.

She is still writing (1935)—but she shows no signs of deserting her Mas des Roses at Mougins. She is settling down. It is the last of a series of houses she has had built for her. It is one of the things we have in common that we are both haunted by a craving for a perfect house somewhere else. In addition to other migrations I built Spade House, half rebuilt Easton Glebe, built Lou Pidou and still find myself a little disturbed by that urge for the impossible perfect home. Her architectural eggs are even more widespread. She has laid a house near Exeter, one near Virginia Water, the Chalet Soleil above Sierre and Mas des Roses.

The period of my life between 1910 and 1913, when Little e was my mistress, corresponds with several novels that were naturally published a little later than the writing. These are *Marriage, The Passionate Friends, The Wife of Sir Isaac Harman,* and *The Research Magnificent.* None of them are among my best work, and one of them, *Bealby*, is a manifest come-down from the level of *Mr. Polly.* They have less sincerity and depth than anything else that I have written. I remember reading parts of *The World Set Free* to her one sunny afternoon on the slopes above Chalet Soleil, and how she fell scolding me and banging at me with her furry gloved hands, because she decided I "*liked* smashing up the world." If Little e had been God the Creator, there would have been no earthquakes, no tigers and no wars, but endless breezes and quite unexpected showers; the flora would not have been without its surprises, a trifle burlesque, but very delicately and variously scented. And there would have been endless furry little animals popping about in the sweet herbage. Little e had an amazing sense of smell. She declared that von Arnim never really smelt right; it was one of her most frequent charges against that "Man of Wrath," and she would come into a room and tell who among her intimates had been there within an hour or so—infallibly.

And while I am recalling these memories of Little e, another incident comes back to me which illustrates the extreme sanity of our relations. There would be a breeze, a quarrel, high words delivered with the utmost literary skill, a stormy departure from the lunch-table in the loggia. Then presently, as I sat and meditated on the extreme unsatisfactoriness of life, Little e would appear, calm and resolute, with a bottle of castor oil and a large table-spoon.

"Good for both of us. Come," she would say, and have no more words about it.

When I was lecturing in America in 1940 I had a long and cheerful letter from her about my last book. She was in Florida. I replied as affectionately, and the next thing I heard of her when I returned to England was that she had died in her sleep.

§5
Rebecca West

While I was in a state of discontent with Little e in the autumn of 1913, a young woman of quite extraordinary quality came into my world. She appeared first as the signature to a number of very witty and boldly written critical articles, in a periodical called *The Free Woman* and elsewhere. (I have told already how Little e and I celebrated an occasion when Rebecca had shocked Mrs. Humphrey Ward.) Rebecca called me "pseudo-scientific" in some attack she made on me, and I asked her to come along and tell me just what she meant by that. She had an aggressive vigour about her that I thought might be used on a better basis of knowledge than she seemed to possess. In asking her to come along, I don't think I had any intention of making love to her. I think that consciously or unconsciously I was imitating Grant Allen's generous gesture to me after my slating of his *Woman Who Did* in 1893.

A young woman came down to lunch at Easton with a curious mixture of maturity and infantilism about her. She had a fine broad brow and dark expressive troubled eyes; she had a big soft mouth and a small chin; she talked well and she had evidently read voraciously—with an excellent memory. We argued and she stood up to my opinions very stoutly but very reasonably. I had never met anything quite like her before, and I doubt if there ever was anything like her before. Or ever will be again. Her real name was Cicely Fairfield; she was of very mixed race; her father was a Scotsman and her mother a music teacher from the West Indies who is described very vividly in the Edinburgh chapter of her book *The Judge*. Rebecca's nervous system was naturally highly strung, but her emotional development had been, I think, further complicated by an ugly encounter with a tramp when she was still only a child. Her father had been an outrageous rake and her mother had a violent anti-sexual bias—stronger even than that of Mrs. Bland or Mrs. Reeves. She wanted to keep her three daughters as successful single women. The eldest was a doctor of medicine and afterwards became a barrister; the second was an M.A. of Edinburgh. Rebecca, the youngest, never graduated; too strenuous schoolwork gave her a spell of brain-fever; and when she recovered she began to write brilliantly. She had a splendid *disturbed* brain; it is evident in all her work.

I did not know anything of her history when we met. I knew her only as an apparently sturdy young woman who made me forget at once that she was only one and twenty. She seemed at once young and mature. After our meeting we exchanged a few notes and she came to see me once in Church Row. I liked her and found her very interesting, but I was on my good behaviour with Little e and we kept the talk bookish and journalistic. Until a visit to Church Row when, face to face with my book-shelves, in the midst of a conversation about style or some such topic, and apropos of nothing, we paused and suddenly kissed each other.

Then Rebecca flamed up into open and declared passion.

It is easy to understand how strong my appeal to her imagination must have been. She was saturated with literary ambition, and my flagrant successfulness must have had a particular glamour for her. My reputation of being a promiscuous lover did me no harm with her. She was under that urgency to get to grips with life that stirs in youthful blood, and she was too critical for commonplace love-making with her contemporaries. She demanded to be my lover and made an accusation of my kiss. It was a promise, she said. I too was by way of thinking that a kiss ought to be a promise. But it was a very unexpected kiss.

I was greatly drawn towards her, and I was held back by my relations to Elizabeth.

Intimations of her excitement crept into her writing. Her mother became aware of her state of mind and carried her off for a holiday in Spain, which abated nothing of her fever. That autumn I was quarrelling with Elizabeth in London. Rebecca and I became lovers.

We had to meet furtively because of the hostility of her mother and sisters. She came to see me at my flat in St. James's Court one afternoon when we were in danger of being interrupted by a valet; it was our second encounter and she became pregnant. It was entirely unpremeditated. Nothing of the sort was in our intention. She wanted to write. It should not have happened, and since I was the experienced person, the blame is wholly mine.

I took lodgings for her at Hunstanton in Norfolk and I lived with her there as much as possible. She went on reviewing and writing. Our son was born on a memorable date, August 4th, 1914, the day of the British declaration of war against Germany. As soon as possible I found a house at Braughing in Herts, a dozen miles or so from Easton, so that I could go to and fro by bicycle or car and, so to speak, live in both places at the same time. There she was installed with a nurse and a housekeeper and there we lived together intermittently for some months.

And when we found ourselves linked by this living tie, we knew hardly anything of each other. We were all, Jane included, taken by surprise. We all wanted to stand by each other as

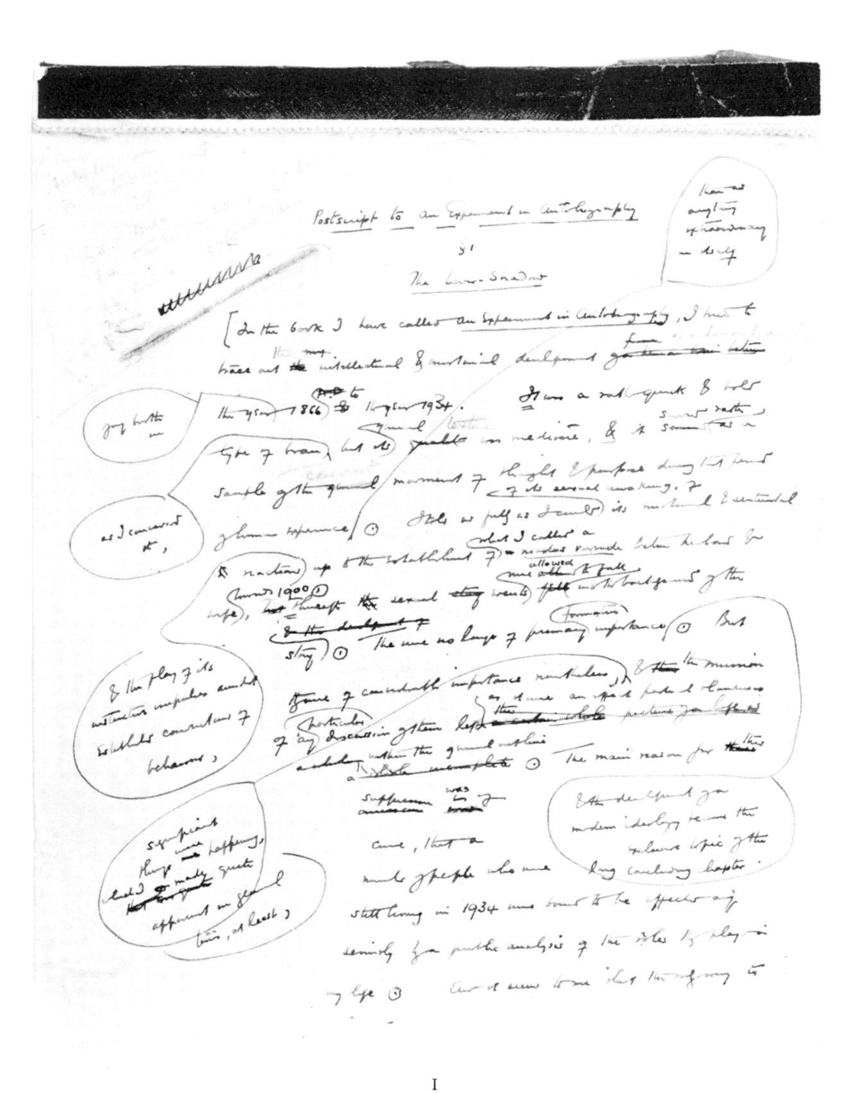

I

H. G. Wells began writing the "Postscript" late in 1934, starting with a tentative contents table jotted down in pencil to guide him

POSTSCRIPT TO AN EXPERIMENT IN AUTOBIOGRAPHY.

On Personal Love

CONTENTS.

§ 1. The Lover-Shadow.

§ 2. The Lover-Shadow across Pimlico and Soho.

§ 3. Dusa.

§ 4. The Episode of little e.

§ 5. Rebecca West. Psychological & Particular.

§ 6. Distress.

§ 7. The Vehement Transit of Odette Keun.

§ 8. Moura.

§ 9. Recessional. Retrospective.

§ 10

§ 11. P. P. S. work in progress

2

A few months later, besides working his way towards the end, he was looking back and revising what he had already written

[A day or so after I found her deceiving me about a small matter of no importance. I reproached her & after her manner she denied the deception [illegible] & we had the last of that long series of quarrels. [illegible] Then I told her my dream of her [illegible] at Tallin. She stood up in my study still defending herself & still refusing me the perfect frankness that alone could have restored our broken confidence & closeness.

[It seemed to me that she was like some lovely animal caught in a net. It was none the less a net about her because it was of her own spinning. She had lost as well as I. I felt as sorry for her as I felt for myself. She had lost as well as I. The things for which she had belittled our love were worthless beside unqualified love that had seemed within our grasp & that had slipped out of our grasp & broken.

[Only the magic has gone out of things for me & there is no more magic, loveliness left for me in my world.

& brightness

["There is no more to be said, my dear," I said with some lasting feeling that still she might do some wonderful thing to save us. But she took it there was no more to be said.

[Because she could not [illegible]

[We kissed & made an end of discussing our unsolved [illegible]. There it lies between us. We are still lovers as the world goes & intimate associates. We can still laugh & talk about a thousand things.

[Dear Moura!

3

Marjorie Wells typed it all from manuscript, of which this is a sample, and often had to do it again after the massacre of her earlier typescripts

272.

free will, not much courage or assertion, but some. More than the fly on the fly-paper has. An increasing amount. And free will is individuality, and individuality is nothing else. Individuality is intrinsic uniqueness and spontaneous initiative. Spontaneous initiative is creation and creation is divinity. And that, I realise, is what I began to say in my first published article, "The Rediscovery of the Unique", in the Fortnightly Review of July 1891, written at Up Park, Petersfield, forty-~~four~~ five years ago.

(July 1st,1935.)

~~Endorsed~~ August 22nd, 1935, October 27th,1935, and again on January 15th, February 5th, March 1st,1936.

THE END.

4
Wells ended "On Loves and the Lover-Shadow" for the first time in May 1935, then for over a year he revised it again and again—about a dozen times. Meanwhile he struggled with *The Anatomy of Frustration* in an effort to express his belief about human living

5
H.G. Wells in maturity

6
Sarah Wells, the writer's mother, at Uppark, Sussex

7
The young Wells

8
Isabel Mary Wells, his cousin, married Wells in 1891

9
Amy Catherine Robbins, later Wells's second wife

10
Amy Catherine Wells,
photographed while they lived
near Folkestone

11
Jane at the Remington,
typing for her husband

12
Wells and his wife and their sons at Spade House

13
Wells and his mother at Spade House

14
H. G. Wells photographed by Jane

15
Wells and Maxim Gorky in St. Petersburg in 1920.
Their interpreter (right) was Moura Budberg

16
Amy Catherine Wells who died in October 1927

17
The author in formal mood

18
At the Commission of Enquiry into the Reichstag Trial, London, 1933

19
H. G. Wells writing

20
Howard Coster's portrait, 1935

21
Dorothy Richardson

22
Violet Hunt

23
Amber Reeves at Newnham College, Cambridge, 1908

24
Elizabeth von Arnim

25
Rebecca West

26
At Lou Pidou: Anthony West, a friend, Odette Keun, Wells

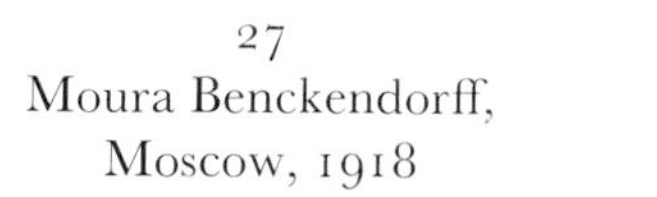

27
Moura Benckendorff,
Moscow, 1918

28
Moura Budberg with Wells
at Brighton, 1935

29
Moura Budberg in old age

30
Wells at the microphone, BBC, January 1943

generously as we could bring ourselves to the situation. Rebecca had never wanted anything but a richly imaginative and sensuous love affair with me, and we had now to attempt all sorts of vaguely conceived emotional adjustments.

We never achieved any adjustment of any sort. We came to like each other extremely and to be extremely exasperated with each other and antagonistic. Rebecca could produce voluminous imaginative interpretations of action and situation that dwarfed my own fairly considerable imaginative fluctuations altogether. We were not left to ourselves. Rebecca had grown up the youngest of the family, with a sort of conceded position of the most gifted and the most hopeful; she grew up in the focus of her mother's and sisters' attention and she had become habituated to their approval and moral support. She needed it even when she defied it, and, whatever she did, was uncertain in her *persona* until they had approved and endorsed it. The intense man-hatred of her mother had imposed itself formally at least on both the elder sisters, so that any lover of Rebecca's would have aroused a family antagonism. And when the strange darling sister fell into an infatuation for a married man with a bad reputation their opposition became hysterically intense. It was just blind opposition; they did nothing to help her. They had no pity for the warmth in her blood and perhaps they were all haunted by the latent possibilities of their own. The elder sister, I am convinced, was distorted by a suppressed jealousy—not for me but for physical love. She adored her sister and also now she hated her.

And whatever we two did, whatever arrangements we made, was spoilt for Rebecca by the relentless and indiscriminating disapproval of her home. They would not let her find any pride in my position and successes; they expressed horror and disgust at any effort we made to face things out together. They forced upon her idiotic lies and pretences; for example, that our Anthony was an "adopted" child; and would not let her be straightforward with her servants in the various ménages we started at Braughing, at Pinner, at Southend-on-Sea and in London. Each in succession was wrecked by them and with no attempt to salvage the situation. They kept up a steady campaign for either complete separation or that I should be divorced and marry her "properly."

Now it is impossible to run a household with a fundamental secret about the relations of its chief members. It is perfectly easy nowadays for unmarried lovers to run a home and find servants who will participate and sympathize; they fall quite easily into that relationship; but to pretend to be married and betray that you are not, or to assume that the frequent familiar man visitor, who creaks so audibly along the passage at night, is a friend or a cousin, seems to arouse a peculiarly violent resentment. If you seem to be ashamed of the situation, your servants, naturally enough, will feel degraded. They will begin to insult or blackmail. Yet if you carry matters with a high hand, they will cheer. And in short Rebecca, whose nature is defiant but whose family loyalty is instinctive, Rebecca, at once a formalist and a rebel, had a very disagreeable time with her servants and her neighbours during the years of our liaison.

We moved our ménage from house to house and from place to place and Anthony was shifted from school to school. Sometimes the Rebecca West who came to see him was his aunt and sometimes his mother and sometimes his adopted mother. Sometimes we two travelled about as lovers and sometimes as friends. Neither of us knew exactly where we were anywhen, and we trailed a web of nervous irritation that twisted about us and strangled the development of the generous liking and affection for each other of which we were certainly capable. Because we did at times love each other very much. We love each other still. We both had streaks of broad humour, strong desires and keen interests, and when these streaks got together we could be very happy. I loved her sense of fun and her imaginative play. The sort of fantasy that got loose in her all too little appreciated book *Harriet Hume* was important to these happy phases.

But the antagonisms carried the day. Her mother and her elder sister never ceased to impress upon her that her position was "inferior" to Jane's. It was really not so very inferior. I went about with her as publicly as she would permit; we dined, lunched and week-ended at friendly country-houses and in very good company. Her good bold talk and her good writing gradually won a place for her of her own. A worthwhile world was willing to tolerate our liaison, provided we acted in concert and did not create needless discords. But she demanded marriage more and more persistently. She developed much the same resentment at Jane's letters that Little e had felt. She could not understand our mutual good-will nor our unconcealed liking. Jane ought to have been weeping her eyes out as an unsuccessful female or "betraying" me in some unpleasant or aggressive fashion with a lover. Rebecca's power of antagonism was far greater than Little e's whimsical hostility and she had a clear purpose in view.

We disputed. I reproached her quite justly with inconsistency. With even greater justice she reproached me with want of consideration for her difficulties. "Tell your family to go hang," said I, "and we can carry London. You set out in life to be a free woman."

"But is it my fault," she asked, "that I have to be a free mother? That wasn't in the bargain."

"We can carry all that. But these attempts at secrecy and putting a false face upon it defeat us."

"Get divorced and marry me."

"Jane is a wife," I argued, "but you could never be a wife. You want a wife yourself—you want sanity and care and courage and patience behind you just as much as I do."

"You've never taken care of me."

"Nor you of me."

It wasn't in our characters. Our quarrelling went on with a score of variations on this perennial dispute. And all the while we had times together when we were happy lovers and the best of company. There was no discord in our physical temperaments or the general liveliness of our minds.

Deeper than these disharmonies of situation, however, there were other divergent forces making for separation. I have already discussed these in general terms in the section of my *Autobiography* (Chapter VIII §5) in which I compare myself with some of my contemporaries. I have faced the facts that my mind is not very vivid in its receptions and that it is obsessed by a necessity to correlate what it apprehends. Rebecca was at the opposite pole to me in both these matters. She saw and felt with an extreme intensity and she could be indifferent to plan and unaware of inconsistencies to an extent that tormented me, so that a considerable antipathy developed between us as writers.

Writing was a serious thing for both of us. I pestered her to make a scheme and estimate a length for the great novel she was writing, *The Judge*, and she grimaced with disgust that I should be compiling an *Outline of History* when I ought to be releasing my imagination in creative literature. She came to hate *The Outline of History* almost as much as she hated Jane. She wanted history to be full of wonderlands. She hated it being written as a picture of developing inter-communication. She did not really believe it could have an "Outline." We wintered together at Amalfi in 1922–23; we went for long walks, made love, made fun of most things, and quarrelled about our writings. She was deep in *The Judge* and I was writing *The Secret Places of the Heart* at her. She found my hero's obsession with fuel a personal offence. It was perhaps a personal offence.

Her handling of *The Judge* was typical of all that I did not admire in her. In 1918 we had spent part of the summer in a *pension* in Maidenhead, and walking in that town one day she saw a judge on his way to the Assizes. He was going to his job with an old-fashioned stateliness, preceded by officials with silver staves. She took a dislike to him.

The encounter jumped into a story in which a soiled and impoverished woman, that same soiled and impoverished woman she had done so beautifully in *The Return of the Soldier*, was to play the chief part. (The original of the woman was the landlady of a lodging we kept in Pimlico, to whom we were both much attached.) There was an old scandal about an English judge who died of a seizure in a brothel, and Rebecca suddenly saw the pompous figure she had encountered in the morning sneaking out incognito into the streets at night after too generous a dinner and picking up our woman—*whose beloved husband he had sentenced to death ten or twelve years before*. She knows him at once, but he is all unaware of what he is following to her lodging. She determines to murder him as he sprawls expectant on her bed; she brings in her bread-knife and suddenly he turns and looks at her, sees the knife in her hand and murder in her eyes, and dies of heart-failure. That was the original story of *The Judge*. But first Rebecca realized that it was necessary to make the reader understand that the crime for which her husband was condemned was a tragic and sympathetic necessity, and also that the woman must have loved her husband heart and soul. She opened her book, very rashly, before husband and wife had met. The rest of this whale of a book, which is full of good writing and reading, displays Rebecca in the steamy rich jungle of her imaginations, trying to fight her way through from a girlhood in Edinburgh and a boyhood in Rio, to *The Judge*. She never got to the Judge. At the end of an immense mass of unequal but often gorgeous writing, she had reached no further than the murder, and there she wound up the book, still keeping the title of *The Judge*, because that had already been announced by her publishers for two years.

I pestered her for three years "Construct, construct,"—until she turned upon me fiercely and called me a "nagging schoolmaster."

She writes like a loom producing her broad rich fabric with hardly a thought of how it will make up into a shape, while I write to cover a frame of ideas. We did harm to each other as writers. She prowled in the thickets and I have always kept close to the trail that leads to the World-State. She splashed her colours about; she exalted James Joyce and D.H. Lawrence, as if in defiance of me—and in despite of Jane and everything trim, cool and deliberate in the world—and I wrote with an ostentatious disregard of decoration; never used a rare phrase when a common one would serve, and was more of a journalist than ever. I find her excursions into general criticism, such as *The Strange Necessity*, pretentious and futile, and she finds the love-making of my later novels incurably theoretical and shallow. Neither of us, I suspect, is absolutely wrong about the other. The love-making in my novels is certainly not there for its own sake; it is a formula in a situation. And generally my novels are psychologically unsubtle.

We gradually detached ourselves and I was more hurt to lose her than she to be quit of me. There was much heat and bad blood between us for a time—we are both impulsive and vividly expressive—all the while that a strong strand of personal attachment either way, though stronger I think from me to her, and habits of familiar association were tugging at us contrariwise.

It would be a tedious story to tell how we disentangled ourselves after the war. If it had not been for the existence of our son Anthony, we should probably have broken sooner. I had gone off on my own to the French and Italian fronts in 1916 (*War on Three Fronts*) and I went to Russia in 1920 (*Russia in the Shadows*). I came back subtly changed from these separations, and something happened to my imagination in Russia of which

I was to reap the full harvest later. I still wanted to go on with the liaison much more than Rebecca did, because plainly it suited my needs much more than it did hers. I found nobody in our immediate world so attractive as she was nor such good company. We abandoned Pimlico. She came up from Leigh-on-Sea and settled in London in a flat in Kensington. I would go to Kensington from my flat in Whitehall Court for long intimate half-days and evenings. We took motoring holidays in the country, going chiefly south and west, and presently we went abroad together. We had a long time together in the south of Italy at Amalfi in 1920, and came back, staying together in Rome. In October 1921 I went to America to write about the Washington Conference, and I returned not to England but to Spain. She joined me at Algeciras and we spent three months there, and visited Seville, Granada and Madrid. In January 1923 we were in Paris. All this time she was chafing at the bonds that held her to me, demanding marriage or a separation, and I was holding on to her. I ought to have liberated her; I realize I got much the best of our relationship; but there was no one to take her place with me, and she was fond of me as well as resentful and there was no one ready to take my place with her.

Under the date of June 20th, 1923, I find in my appointments diary the only note I have of a queer little interlude that for a time, oddly enough, seemed to link Rebecca and myself more closely. Somewhen in April or May a slight and very pretty young woman with a face like the *Mona Lisa* came from Vienna to London and demanded to see me to tell me about the terrible state of affairs then prevailing in Austria. I was interested by her letter, and she came to tea with Jane and myself at Whitehall Court. She told us of the many harassing things that were happening to the educated and professional people of Vienna, and she asked permission to translate my book on Sanderson, the Oundle headmaster, into German.

Her father, it seemed, was a keen educationist; there was no particular enthusiasm on the part of German publishers for the book, and I gave her a provisional consent to the experiment. This provided her with an excuse to call again in order to ask for the elucidation of various allusions. Her next visit fell when Jane was away at Easton. She passed rather suddenly and skilfully from an intelligent appreciation of my educational views to passionate declarations. I have always felt a certain dislike for the rôle of Joseph; a vulgar and shabby shame indeed of discretion; moreover I hate to snub an exile in distress, and she was an extremely appetizing young woman. After which event she was established as a very inconvenient little secret in my life. She wanted me; she plied me with love-letters and professed an unendurable passion. She had stimulated my senses and I assuaged her sufferings on various occasions—vowing each time that there should be no more of this. She came down for a week-end at Felsted near Easton and asked me to call one afternoon in my car to meet her hosts, a schoolmaster and his wife—whom she represented as great admirers of my work. When I went over I found they had gone away and left her to mind the house until they returned. She was minding it in a tea-gown and little else.

"This must end," said I, "this must end"—allowing myself to be dragged upstairs.

She went back to Austria very reluctantly. I corresponded with her about the translations and suddenly she took it into her head that she had not been decisive enough; that her affair with me was capable of development upon an altogether handsomer scale.

She turned up again upon the telephone in London. "I've come back," she announced, but by this time I had thought over this betrayal of Rebecca—I had excused it to myself on the score of some flirtation of Rebecca with Sinclair Lewis—and I had resolved to stop the liaison. I refused to see her, and, since she had a habit of calling unexpectedly at Whitehall Court, I gave my maid instructions that she should not be admitted. I felt absurdly on the defensive about it, yet there was nothing else to be done.

One evening as I was dressing for dinner I heard someone come into my study. She had come to the flat and by ill-luck my proper housemaid was out that night and her place had been taken by another girl who had let her in. I went into my study dressed for dinner and found the young lady on my hearth-rug. She was wearing a water-proof, which she flung open, revealing herself naked except for shoes and stockings.

"You must love me," she said, "or I will kill myself. I have poison. I have a razor."

I perceived myself in a corner. She meant to make a tremendous scene. Was I to struggle with her for the poison and the razor? And suppose I hurt her! I realized that the less things happened without witnesses the better for me.

I opened the door wide, called to the maid and told her to telephone down for the hall-porter, who was, I knew, a thoroughly sane and trustworthy man. I had to shout down the passage to her because I did not want to leave the lady by herself in my room. But while my back was turned, she produced an old razor and, before I realized this and could get across the room to her, she had cut herself deeply across the wrists and armpits. I got the razor from her and put her in a chair, bleeding profusely, and when I had satisfied myself that no poison was in evidence, I went to get cold water to stop the bleeding. "Let me die," she cried repeatedly in a voice that was strong enough to be reassuring about the gravity of her injuries. "I love him. I love him."

The hall-porter appeared with remarkable promptitude, and he might have been a trained attendant upon mental cases, so competent was his handling of the situation. Two policemen were summoned. All three of these men were as gravely sympathetic with me as though romantic young women with razors were as common a nuisance as influenza, and, in remarkably little time, she was borne off to Charing Cross Hospital, still stoutly asserting her incurable passion for me.

I returned to my study. My carpet looked like three suicides. My shirt and cuff were smeared with blood. I looked at my watch and found my dinner-party, which was with Montagu, the Secretary of State for India, had been going on for three-quarters of an hour. I telephoned my excuses and sat down to face the situation.

If anyone in the police or press who disliked me got hold of this affair, it was going to get a very disagreeable publicity. But it was just as probable that police and press might prove friendly. It was one of those situations when any funk or flight would cause disaster.

Press and police did prove friendly. I consulted my friend Lord Beaverbrook and he and Lord Rothermere issued an order to all the papers they controlled that "H. G. Wells is not news" for a fortnight. All the London hospitals are haunted by reporters and one or two pressmen rushed off with wild hopes of a scoop. But there was no announcement of "Tragic Affair in Flat of Prominent Author" upon the placards next day, and after a flash of publicity in the *Westminster Gazette* and the *Star* and in the foreign press, the incident vanished from the public mind. People rubbed their eyes and concluded they had never seen that flash.

The police behaved with intelligent stolidity. The hospital authorities were warned to keep reporters off the patient, and they made a few enquiries and came along to me, bringing all the evidence with them. (I also had an interesting conversation with Lady Astor who after her manner was conducting investigations of her own. For Lady Astor in spite of much disregard was for many years—how shall I put it?—the moral custodian of London.) Some years before, I learnt, the young woman had attempted suicide—in the apartments of a British attaché in Vienna. It was her formula. Somewhere—perhaps in a war hospital—she had learnt to cut her veins without the risk of mortal injury. It robbed the affair of its romantic halo but it made it much more manageable for everyone. She had made herself liable to prosecution for attempting suicide, the police told her, but they preferred her to leave the country. She had no relatives or friends in England and it fell to me to play the legal rôle of "best friend;" guarantee her good behaviour and ensure her return to Vienna. And we had to buy a new carpet for my study.

Her love evaporated and I heard no more from her directly. But I was told she had married and all was well with her.

I note (July 1937) that on my seventieth birthday I had a pleasant letter from her. She is happily married and living in England. Since then I have met her and her husband and given her some useful advice about publishing a novel.

This incident would be irrelevant here, were it not for the sidelights it throws on my relations with Rebecca in 1923.

I remember sitting with her in Kensington Gardens on the morning after the scene in my flat with the crisis hanging portentously over us. (Because I found the young woman, in the rôle of a literary admirer and possible interviewer, had visited Rebecca the previous day—I suppose with the idea of staging a triangular situation.) I remember it because it was a good day for us two. So often had we attacked each other with unjust interpretations and unreasonable recriminations that it matters very much to my memories that we sat and talked and were very sane and wise. We arranged to squash all interviewers and all impertinent enquiries; we lunched conspicuously together at the Ivy that day and we carried on. On the whole people who had heard of the business thought it wiser not to speak about it to us.

We carried on through that summer. I spent part of July with her in Marienbad, where she took a cure, on my way to visit President Masaryk at Topolcany in Slovenia, and most of September we were in Swanage with our son and his nurse. We seem to have made several excursions by road into the South-West and Wales. We had the usual moody alternations of lively interest, affection and discord. We loved each other in bright flashes; we were mutually abusive; we were fundamentally incompatible.

The effective break came from her. She signed a contract for a lecturing tour in America in October 1923, and we parted with the clear intention of a separation. In America she formed new friendships and fresh relationships; she had various adventures, and became a self-reliant woman. I found life in London dull without her—and there was little consolation in a few minor infidelities. I don't like incidental infidelities; it is a mate I have always been after. Jane wanted to go with the boys into the Alps for winter sport, and my lungs were no longer comfortable in the high air. So that winter I went to the sunshine of the Estoril near Lisbon and found the Galsworthys staying at the next hotel. I struck up an intimacy with a very pleasant red-haired widow who had come with a brother-in-law to see about a monument to her husband who had died suddenly in Lisbon the year before. We went for long walks together; we played tennis with Galsworthy; we were presently giving joint lunch- and dinner-parties and we made love. She had been brought up in a vicarage and married at nineteen to a typical army man, greatly her senior. They had spent the summers attending race-meetings in England and the winters gambling modestly but firmly on the Riviera. So that our worlds were poles asunder and we found a vast amount to talk about. We parted in April at St. Jean-de-Luz and we have ever since been very good friends. She is one of those women who go on quietly frittering away their resources by attempts to supplement them by bright little unsound furniture shops and millinery shops and so forth—and she is still a very cheerful and gallant lady. We lunch together—about once a year.

I met Jane in Paris in April on my way back from the Estoril, and we stayed there a week or so and then I returned to England.

Now I ought never to have gone to Lisbon. I ought never to have returned to England. I had fallen in love, more completely and sincerely than I had ever done before, in Russia in 1920. I ought to have gone after that woman in 1923, so soon as I broke with Rebecca. I will try to clear up why I did not do so, when I tell more particularly of that affair.

Rebecca and I were both back in London that spring. We were both acutely aware of each other's existence; attracted by old associations and sulky and angry. I made love to my widow and one or two other people; my interests were in fragments, and I was intensely discontented with myself. I really wanted Rebecca—with a difference—very intensely; and she still wanted me—with a difference also. Considerable differences in both cases. It wasn't so easy for either of us to break away. The world was full of men she couldn't talk to as she talked to me, and of women I had only a brief and simple use for. We came together once or twice and then she went off to Austria with our son Anthony and some friends. I found England full of heart-ache and I resolved to go off by myself round the world. I wish I had gone to Naples where my Russian friend, Moura Budberg, was living, as the secretary of Maxim Gorky, and looked at her again. But she had come out of Russia in 1921; she had married a Baltic baron, Baron Budberg, and divorced him, and I imagined she was Gorky's mistress. I did not suppose there was much left of our flash of intense passion in 1920. Yet we corresponded; "Dear Moura," "Dear H.G." We wrote occasional vague guarded letters to each other. Neither of us seemed quite certain about the real and enduring value of what had happened. We doubted whether there was anything more to happen between us and yet we could not leave each other alone altogether.

At Geneva I went through a strange mental phase. Although I was very busy indeed and meeting a great variety of people; attending the Assembly; going to lunches and dinners; giving a party; taking my friend Mrs. Tom Lamont for excursions across the lake in a motor-boat; supping in France with George Mair or on the Salève with this or that little group, I was secretly in the intensest misery and haunted to an extraordinary extent by the thought of Rebecca. At that time I was feeling too acutely to observe myself. But I see now that Rebecca had become for me the symbol of the Lover-Shadow and that I was unable to conceive of it in any other form than hers—or exist without it. I began to see her on balconies, away across restaurants. Any dark-haired woman would become Rebecca for me. I felt I must at any cost get her back to me and get back to her. I sent her a telegram to Austria suggesting we should go to Montpellier for the winter with Anthony, and make another try at life together. But Rebecca was now inflexibly in revolt. More things than I knew of were to make our reunion impossible, and she telegraphed her refusal. That came almost simultaneously with an eager voice on the telephone.

"Who are you?" said I.

"Odette—Odette Keun. I've written you so often."

"What do you want?"

"I've come all the way up from Grasse to see you. I want you to come to my hotel."

I thought at the telephone.

"I'll come," I said, after a pause.

How I went and what happened I will tell in the next section. That voice on the telephone marked the onset of an adventure sufficiently vivid and exciting to release me from my obsession with Rebecca. My heart was like a nascent element at that time, ready and urgent for some new combination. And all unknown to me, that Moura I had loved in 1920, and was destined to love again, was in Vienna, and altogether ready and willing for a reunion with me. I had nothing to do then to regain her but to go across Switzerland to her. If I had known. You can get a glimpse of her at that very time in chapter 6 of Bruce Lockhart's *Retreat from Glory*. But five troubled years were to elapse before I was to set eyes on her again—and feel again the peculiar magic she has always had for me. She had stirred among the ashes of an old affair with him—which is told very frankly in his *Memoirs of a British Agent*—and she had found not a spark left alive in them.

But I cannot close this chapter on Rebecca without a word or two about the peculiar wit that made her companionship at its best the warmest, liveliest and most irreplaceable of fellowships. She filled our intimate world with fantasies and nicknames. She kept, for example, an imaginary public-house and she was the missus and I drove a gig. There were times when we almost materialized that gig. Or we were two melancholy but furry and eccentric animals, the Pussteads. Or she was a fantastic mixture of herself and Emma Goldman and Violet Hunt; she gave lectures upon refined subjects and had startling indelicate lapses, and in that shape she was called, I forget now why, the "Legendary Panther." We would concoct long passages of a lecture or conversation by the Legendary Panther in which she struggled phrase after phrase, with unavailing snatches at circumlocutions and evasive allusions, towards the ultimate unavoidable shock. Her speech gravitated towards indecency as inevitably as the tradesmen's play in *A Midsummer Night's Dream*. The Legendary Panther found bishops irresistible at dinner-parties. Her archness then exceeded that of a Roman aqueduct, as she advanced towards them. She tried a peculiar innuendo with them that never failed to break down. She went across life in the same sweeping fashion. She was a great invention. And none of it was ever written down, alas! Most of the fun in Rebecca is lost for ever.

Apart from our fantasies—you get something of their quality in her charming book, *Harriet Hume*—she had queer flashes of a lurid inimitable wit. Here I will recall only two of her flashes.

Someone said that Cecil Chesterton, who had a dingy complexion, was really a very clean person. It was not dirt at all. When he bathed at Le Touquet, he came out of the water just as grey-blue as when he went in.

"But did you look at the Channel?" said Rebecca.

Robert Lynd was a drooping dark Irishman with the opposition temperament and a plaintive voice. Sylvia, his wife, caught something of the Celtic sadness and enjoyed indifferent health. "It comes of sleeping with a damp husband," said Rebecca.

§6

Psychological and Parental

This Postscript does not tell the main story of my life. It is the story of a broad strand in my life that had to be turned away from the reader in the original *Experiment in Autobiography*. Let that fact, that this "Postscript" is an addendum, be kept in the picture. All the main lines of my development were given in the *Autobiography* except for one suppression; that the Lover-Shadow by which my *persona* was sustained was no longer definitely represented in it after 1900. The careless reader was left to suppose and almost lured to suppose that the loyal support and affection of Jane and my own conceit of myself was sufficient to sustain my nervous and imaginative balance. The more observant caught a glimpse in occasional admissions and allusions and flashes of light between the lines; of affairs that were not merely refreshment but also imaginative excursions and revivifications. This "Postscript," with its theory of the Lover-Shadow, exposes all that censored strand of activity.

There is no separating psychological and physical—in my make-up at any rate—and all these "love affairs" in my life have this in common, that they are attempts—or at any rate were, in certain phases, attempts—to embody and concentrate the Lover-Shadow in any other human being. It is not every brain that is as disposed to concentrate the Lover-Shadow as much as I have been, and it is not everyone who links the Lover-Shadow as closely to a sexual relationship as I have done. Since I am very much a body as well as a mind, all these love affairs have sought a physical expression; and since I am ineradicably heterosexual, they have never been loves or intimate friendships with men; they have always been love-relations with women. My world is full of friendly men, allies and associates, but none of them has ever become in any way *necessary* and apparently irreplaceable as a fixated Lover-Shadow becomes. The loss of none of them could have produced the same effect of a lost background.

I doubt if there is any difference except in degree and proportion between the man and the woman in this matter of a Lover-Shadow. I suppose that while I was trying to embody my Lover-Shadow in Jane, or afterwards, with reservations, in Amber or Rebecca, my mistress also was trying, with whatever strength of egotism she had, to embody her Lover-Shadow in me. My long struggle with Rebecca was obviously the fight of two very wilful people to compel each other to accept the conditions of an uncongenial Lover-Shadow.

Our telegrams between Austria and Geneva ended all thought of further intimacy between us. We corresponded and met at times about our son's affairs, but with a faint flavour of resentment always. When she wrote her worst book, *The Strange Necessity*, I wrote to her unkindly about it. For her good, of course. But I had better have written kindly or not at all. Her writing is in a different world from mine.

In 1931 (if I remember rightly) she invited herself to tea with me one day. We were easy and friendly with each other; we talked about our son's work, and then she told me she was going to marry. I thought it was a sisterly thing to come and tell me, and it warmed my heart to her. She married and she married happily, and she and her husband took a flat in Orchard Court at the other end of Baker Street to Chiltern Court. He is an able business man; he admires her unreservedly; and she can live with him without the perpetual friction of antagonistic mental disposition and conflicting literary ambitions. Our relations have mellowed more and more.

Meanwhile our son has grown up to be a very good friend of mine and of his half-brothers and half-sister. I have never detected any trace of jealousy between these four on account of their differences in legal status. All four of these new individualities have developed gifts and qualities of their own and to my great satisfaction are living honourably in this difficult phase of human history. But I will not pursue them to draw them into my autobiography. They mean much to me in friendliness, interest and happiness, but they do not go deeply into the living structure of my Self. They go on with their own relationships and mine are an older system. Sons and daughters nowadays are still an intimate part of one's pride, a projected part of one's *persona*, but no more part of one's Lover-Shadow —than is the general world of acquaintances and friends. Occasionally, almost shyly, they will talk of my work, or of what they are doing, to me, and conversely, and even more shyly, I will advise or criticize. With punctilio. I happen to have collaborated with both G. P. and F. R. Wells—with G. P. in the *Science of Life* and with F. R. in the making of films— but we have done our work together with exactly the same freedoms and civilities that would have prevailed between congenial collaborators who had no kinship with one another. This detachment has come about not so much of set intention as by a natural disposition. I had what I suppose is a perfectly natural emotional excitement when I had my first-born son; and in *The Passionate Friends* (1913) when Gip, the eldest, was twelve or thirteen, I find myself discussing fatherhood and sonship. We happen to form a quite loyal and mutually helpful group, and both my daughters-in-law have adapted themselves very cordially to this association. Marjorie Craig, who was my secretary before she married my son Gip and who is still one of my two secretaries, has been as it were the business nucleus for us all. We all rely on each other and trust each other. But all that is a matter of free association and preference and interest. What I am writing of here is the psychological inter-penetration and mutual service of *personas* and Lover-Shadows. I think we should feel something embarrassingly incestuous about the idea of any such response.

Maybe in the past the family concentration was psychologically more intimate and entangled; and the atmosphere of ideas in which my children have grown up may be exceptionally *modern*, with a real antagonism to emotional concentrations and a far more definite reference and mental orientation towards a socialist world-community than is general. We do not like concentration of feeling and we do not like being tied. It is another aspect in my family of that organic claustrophobia in my own make-up that I have discussed in my main *Autobiography*. Clustering is antipathetic to us. I have always been disposed to despise people who cluster close in families, gangs, clans and nations. That is my main objection to Jews. And Scotsmen. And the provincial French. I reveal perhaps the immunizing influence of a serum drawn from the very disease, when I say that roughly speaking the English have not this human disposition to remain clustered so highly developed. It is my theory that a world socialism means a bolder and more fearless individualism; the courage to advance in open order; I am working my way towards that freedom in this attempt to define and analyse the limitations of the Lover-Shadow; and it is interesting to find myself coming unexpectedly upon the same conclusion that my sexual experiences open out, apropos of my children.

§7
THE VOCIFEROUS TRANSIT OF ODETTE KEUN

I SUPPOSE I ought to write of Odette Keun as a Bad Woman, and in a strain of resentment and hostility. She was, from certain points of view, a thoroughly nasty and detestable person; vain, noisy and weakly outrageous. But I know one or two good things about her which are difficult for other people to know— a very real thread of unhappiness and self torment in her make-up—and that knowledge by itself qualifies my dislike. And also there was a strand of warped but very intense affectionateness in her. She excited me a good deal; she made me laugh and, for all her spasmodic efforts to do so, she never really hurt me. She wanted to do so at times extravagantly, but the claws never got into my eyes. As I spin my memories of her about, I realize that, if it were not for the compunction I feel for her pitifulness, she would be beyond all question the Greatest Lark I have ever had. If only she had had a spring of that deep laughter which fuses minds I might be living with her now.

But she was protected by an invincible barrier from her own sense of humour. She was immensely vain. She could not bear to think that she was ridiculous. She could not bear the thought of being laughed at. And there was no going back on anything she had done. Her wildest extravagances had to be taken seriously; taken with hushed respect, as significant parts of an unparalleled consistent whole. She had to be the great, magnificent, intricate, wonderful, potent and focal Odette Keun—and she fought poisonously for that; until she made her very animal pets detest and run away from her. She was indeed not sane; she was crazy with vanity, with the cruellest vindictiveness if ever her vanity was bruised. Periodically she was mad, I think; certifiably mad. I did my best for her—though it was a clumsy best—as I realized this. I felt I had so far cheated her as to acquiesce in the theory that we were lovers, and I believed that if anyone could save her from ending in entire loneliness it was I. But as the evil in her grew stronger, I could endure her no more. I had realized that I loved that Moura, of whom I will presently tell, and that made everything more difficult.

Odette was the daughter of the head dragoman in the Dutch Legation at Constantinople, and it was characteristic of her that she always said she had been brought up not in a legation but in an embassy. Her father, she told me, was also a creature of intense vanity and vehemence. He was insanely philo-progenitive and had a number of illegitimate children. He nourished a grievance that he was not promoted to the Dutch Diplomatic Service, and at last he went mad outright at a banquet; delivered a speech of threats and boastings, and was carried off raving to die.

Odette's mother was an Italian widow and Keun's second wife. She also had a violent temper. The ménage was run chiefly by Greek servants and it included a half-brother, a half-sister and an illegitimate half-sister, who had been adopted, as well as Odette's two younger sisters. She was brought up in an atmosphere of screams, recriminations and beatings. Outside the walls of the great garden was the Constantinople of Abdul Hamid, with its pariah dogs, its dangerous filthy streets, its chronic disposition to massacre Armenians.

At that time the British had set up a girls' school in Constantinople under a certain Miss Green, and to this girls went from all the embassies and legations, the children of prosperous merchants and shipping-agents, and a miscellany of Levantines. Miss Green was an energetic teacher; Odette was quick-witted and one of the brightest of her pupils, and she learnt English and French extremely well. She had acquired modern Greek from the servants, with a store of rich colloquialisms, and she had a fair knowledge of German and some Italian and Turkish. The school, like all Constantinople, reeked with international rivalry and with the intensest snobbery. Odette, snubbed by the coldly arrogant English and the aggressively arrogant Germans, found her revenge in the schoolwork. She was a voracious reader with an excellent memory. When Keun died, leaving very little provision for his family, Miss Green kept his three daughters in the school at nominal fees—but exacted a certain unspecified assistance from them that Odette resented bitterly.

So far she had never had a chance of acquiring any sort of poise. Her one steadying influence was the rather harsh affection of Miss Green. To that she responded fitfully. She also developed a shrewish protective affection for her younger sisters. But poverty, the unending humiliation of social inferiority and disadvantage, a wild desire to be and enjoy and triumph were too much for her flimsily balanced nervous disposition. Her behaviour became outrageous. Not sexually. She was too fiercely distressed for love-making. She ran away from home to wander in Asia Minor across the Bosporus while she was still in her teens. She was brought back and scolded by the Dutch Consul, whose face she slapped. Face-slapping, among these Constantinople girls, seems to have been considered a very gallant high-spirited conclusive retort to reproof. After much consultation and coming and going, she was packed off to an Ursuline convent in Holland.

In this convent she did well. It was the first bit of continuous orderly living she had ever had. She had done orderly work in Miss Green's school, but then she had been coming and going to the fever of her home, and she had had the slights and bickering of her fellow pupils to keep her in reaction. Hitherto she had been a Presbyterian, after the religion of her father, but the order, the austere calm and a certain sweetness in the convent life gave her a new conception of Christianity and of human possibility. She worked hard and secured some sort of diploma that endorsed the fact that she had had a good schooling. Schooling she had, but not education; I never knew anyone so well informed and narrowly ignorant as she was. She learnt quickly, remembered brightly and never synthesized.

I do not know the exact order of events in her life during the next few years. She has told it all over to me in fragments, and I have never before tried to set it out in order. All this I have related happened to her before 1914. The main fact was her conversion to Catholicism and her admission to a house of Dominican nuns at Tours. She had returned from Holland to Constantinople with this in her mind, but she was not free to carry out her intentions until she was twenty-one. She conceived a great disgust for the social life to which she had come back. She and her sisters were too poor to make good marriages after the Levantine pattern and, in spite of the stir in her blood, her disposition was too quickly resentful for her to give herself to a lover. She seems to have had an itch to write from an early age; her ambition had been fostered by Miss Green, and now she produced a short novel, *Mesdemoiselles Daisne de Constantinople* (1916). It was a transcript of the love affairs of her sisters and, with an unpremeditated veracity, it reflects the Levantine atmosphere of base tittle-tattle and unscrupulous accusation in which they were living. The disposition to be sarcastic; to "show up" everybody and everything; to feel the power of the pen by hurting and humiliating, is very evident. I cannot judge how much this disposition in Odette was due to the poison in her little world and how far it was due to the poison in her blood. Two ingredients may have met in her. The spirit of scurrilous society journalism contrived somehow to be Odette's Fairy Godmother.

There is the element of the abusive letter in everything Odette has ever published and, over and above her published writings, she has become by choice and habit an abusive letter-writer. She radiates abusive letters to people she knows and people she does not know. They vary between mere threat and filth and shrewd comment; she speaks of them as psychological studies; and she finds, in writing them, a solace, a reassurance, a sense of authoritative judgment that nothing else can give. She cannot, as literary people say, "write;" nevertheless she is a born writer. You cannot realize Odette Keun unless you figure her intent, absorbed, scribbling away for dear life, fluent, unhesitating, in pencil because it goes faster. Then off to the post before the scanty afterthoughts give trouble.

Sometimes I am a little disposed to speculate how far my own "expressiveness" is not akin to Odette's inky issue. I think there is a difference in quality, but the same "Strange Necessity," as Rebecca would call it, seems to drive us. "Get up and state it;" the urgency is the same in her brain and mine. I can see the self-protective need in her that makes her get up and state it all wrong. But I cannot see what self-protective need may be at work in myself.

So Odette was already a writer when she took her plunge into the nunnery. She spent two years there and she was turned out. Mother Church is a wary old bird; her organization, grimly on the defensive against a perpetually renewed modernity, needs willing instruments and not difficult souls, and Odette remained a novice until her rejection.

She was disgusted with all human lovers, she declared, and

for a time she set her heart on the Supreme Lover, Christ. Her Lover-Shadow concentrated on him. He would listen, He would understand, possibly even He would respond. But some realistic strain in her, or an excessive impatience, prevented her from developing into an ecstatic saint. She was accorded no visions. She began to be horribly bored. There were no signs that the love of Christ for her was undergoing any responsive concentration. She fell foul of the Mother Superior upon petty matters of discipline and routine.

She began to develop "Doubt." She had read something about Evolution in Holland and she made herself interesting to her Confessor with a string of obvious difficulties. She was a bright thing among nuns and very much alive, and he was an ambitious young man. He found wrestling with her perplexities quite the most stimulating part of his duties.

He wrestled manfully. Talks of a great spiritual friendship crept into their encounters. She might become another Saint Teresa and be a power in the Church. One day he kissed her on the forehead and later he kissed her on the lips. Then he was overwhelmed with dismay and went and owned up to *his* Confessor.

The Church has a greater need for able preachers than for doubting and temperamental nuns, and Odette was thrown out ruthlessly and brutally. She found herself in Paris with the clothes she had brought into the convent and little else. Mother Church made it perfectly clear to her that it did not care a damn (which is here quite the appropriate word) for its erring transitory child. By the disciplines of the Order she had not looked in a mirror for two years. She saw herself in one in the railway station waiting-room and did not know herself, so pallidly fat had the convent fare made her.

She got into touch with a married sister in Paris, but I do not know the precise sequence of events. The war was going on, and I think she did some amateurish nursing. She was resuming her outward flow of letters and projecting a tremendous novel or "show up" of the Catholic Church. In some way she met a professor of sociology in Lille University, Bernard Lavergne. He was of a good wealthy Protestant family; and he had read her first book and been attracted by it. He was married, but he proposed to Odette to become his mistress. She agreed, and her perhaps unwholesomely preserved chastity came to an end. Not without difficulty.

I am tempted here to an excursion upon the mental and moral consequences of prolonged virginity in the case of imaginative, nervously active people. It is an aspect of sexual psychology still to be worked out (1934). As a rule prolonged virginity means no real ascetic purity. Sexual pleasure—when it does not take the mind out of itself—leads to intense self concentration. A furtive sexual system grows up detached from the general activities. It does not appease the normal demands of vanity. Release may come too late. This, I think, is what explains much that is perplexing in the life of G. B. Shaw; and it goes far to explain Odette Keun. Essentially they are masturbators. With me she led a normal sexual life; but occasionally, because of some quarrel, or because I was away from her, or because of the periodic disturbances of life, the old system of habits asserted itself and with that a sort of secondary personality took control of her. Her face and complexion changed for the worse. Then it was she was most self-assertive, most vindictive and treacherous, most prone to the "show up" ideal of writing.

Lavergne was not very much in the way of a lover. He had war work to do in Algiers and he took her with him. She attempted medical and nursing work with the Arab women but not very successfully. Ultimately she became pregnant by Lavergne and had an abortion. She was too narrowly made for child-bearing. Then she fell flamingly in love with a French officer and left Lavergne for him. Lavergne behaved with great generosity, being indeed immensely relieved to find his affair at an end. Men in garrison are susceptible, but French Catholic officers draw a hard line between a mistress and a wife; and presently the young officer, finding an adequate *dot*, broke off from her and married. Odette exploded with a novel which was supposed to hold him up to pitiless ridicule and display herself in a brilliant light, *Une Femme Moderne* (1919). It was dedicated to me, "A H. G. Wells. Tu nous as imposé tes songes," but I have never had the curiosity to read it. It was a second release of what I may call her "pitiless pen" complex.

Thereafter she returned to Paris; went to Rome; picked up with some Italian representative who was going to Georgia, and went to Tiflis. Vehement fluctuations of relationship ensued, and something of it was embalmed in her romance, *Prince Tariel*, now suppressed on account of a quite wanton libel the "pitiless pen" complex had worked into it. The Bolsheviks were coming into Georgia at that time and Odette found herself returning to Constantinople with a crowd of other nondescripts upon a refugee ship. The British were then in control; they were doing the job with their customary heaviness; and for no justifiable reason, and in complete disregard of her appeals to call in this or that person she had known in Constantinople, they packed her off with a number of other unfortunates to the Crimea. There she was at once arrested as a British agent trying to get into the country in the rôle of a deported suspect. She had the better part of a year before she could get out of the enquiring grip of the Ogpu, and she emerged with the material for what is perhaps her best and most amusing book, *Sous Lénine*.

Somewhen in 1923 Middleton Murry asked me to notice the English translation of this in his magazine, the *Adelphi*; I did so favourably, expressing my opinion that she was a Lark, and this produced a copious letter from her. I was the hero of her life, she said. Miss Green had talked of me; she had carried

The Outline of History into Georgia with her; she had already dedicated a book to me, and some day she hoped to meet me face to face. Other letters followed with a note of increasing personal urgency—I had acquired no discretion from the adventure of the young Austrian woman—and I replied briefly but amiably. There was libellous matter in the English version of *Sous Lénine*, *My Adventures in Bolshevik Russia*, but I did not observe that.

Most of this history I have given was of course quite unknown to me at the time our correspondence began. She was an ex-Dominican novice who had taken to writing and adventure and had been to Georgia and Russia, and that was all I knew about her. I found her letters good fun, though fun on the copious side. She was very much on her good behaviour with me in those days. She tried to bring matters to a climax in 1923 with a long letter from Paris. She was at loose ends, she had nothing to live for. Would I come to Paris and "take" her before she died? All she asked for was two or three days to make me happy. Then *nunc dimittis*. As I have confessed, I have an irrational dread of the Joseph rôle. But I replied that, as everyone in the small world of the intelligentsia knew, I happened to be the lover of Rebecca West and was all for loyalty in these matters. She replied in a strain of equal nobility—and for a time her letters became less frequent.

But they resumed in 1924. I was evidently filling the rôle of her Lover-Shadow; and she imagined me—as she had imagined Christ before me—greatly intrigued by the qualities of the personality she was displaying. She had a discursive intelligence that splashed widely. Sometimes she was acute; generally she was—how shall I say it?—brightly obvious; always she was copious. I answered occasionally and briefly. She was living in a small lodging at Magagnosc near Grasse, which she described very attractively; she aspired to some rôle in life that eluded her. In August I sent her a card saying I was going on an unplanned journey round the world, beginning at Geneva. Everybody, I said, had occasionally to readjust in life; it wasn't only her problem. And just then she heard from Paris that I was breaking with Rebecca for good. She acted with precipitation. She packed a bag and made for my Geneva address. Which brings me to the point I reached at the end of §6.

She had instructed the hotel people to send me up to her room, and I found myself in a dimly lit apartment with a dark slender young woman in a flimsy wrap and an aroma of jasmine. She flung herself upon me with protests of adoration. I was all she had to live for. She wanted to give her whole life to me. She wanted nothing but to be of service to me.

"If you feel like *that*," said I. . . .

I think at the time Odette made her protestation in absolute good faith. She really was confused and dismayed by life and, just as she had thought to thrust the responsibility for her conduct upon the Catholic Church, so now she turned to me to become the protecting, sustaining, responsive, understanding Lover-Shadow for her greedy and frustrated *persona*. It was the call for the lover that we all make—with an egoistic intensity that was all her own. In form she gave; in effect she grabbed.

This sort of free gift is one that no one should accept. I did my best to accept it. I did not fall in love with Odette, though I found her exciting and attractive. I thought only of myself in the matter. My life was restless and incomplete. I wanted, hidden away in the sunshine, a home to which I could retreat from England and work in peace. I wanted someone to keep house for me—and I wanted a mistress to tranquillize me and companion me. She would be *there*. She would never come to Paris or London with me or invade my English life. I would keep her and provide for her. She too would write and be free to do as she chose when I was away. I put the thing to her quite brutally, and she professed to be overjoyed at my proposal. We could not meet openly in Geneva; and my time was filled with engagements. I gave her a day on the lake in a canoe; spent a night at her hotel, and sent her back to Magagnosc to wait for me there.

A few days afterwards I joined her. She was living in a shabby lodging in a village, and I stayed in a boarding-house close by; but she knew of a furnished house to let, Lou Bastidon, near Malbosc; and she knew of a woman who would cook for us. We walked down to the house and tried its possibilities, and I met the projected cook, Félicie Goletto, whom I found an altogether delightful woman. I arranged to take the house and spend the winter with Odette, and I went back to London to gather my things together.

Lou Bastidon is the "Villa Jasmin" in *The World of William Clissold*. Clementina, as you see her in the chapter called "Irruption of Mimosa," is an aspect, a gay and not very exaggerated impression, of Odette at the early stage. We had nearly three years in the house altogether and they were fairly pleasant and successful years. While I was there in winter, Jane would take a holiday in the Alps with the boys, and in summer we distributed our summer holidays; Jane in Scotland or abroad, and I with Odette writing amidst the olives. Life went pleasantly at Easton and in London, and at Lou Bastidon Odette and I scribbled and disputed and went for long walks and saw few people. She would bewail my departures and go off to Paris to her sisters, or she she would go off alone in an exploratory spirit to Algiers. I played the lover to her; I played at times with some conviction; she came near to being contented with her lot. She worked upon a novel about her convent experiences that promised well, and I was as nearly in love with her as I ever became. I like playing the lover and I suppose in my letters to her—which she is always wanting to sell and which ultimately she will sell—it is in this period that they come nearest to being love-letters.

She had the crudest ideas about money values; I wanted to live simply, and at Lou Bastidon, I suppose, we lived upon less than five hundred a year all told. She practised "economies" with great gusto; kept her accounts meticulously, and was dismayed when I bought her dresses in Nice and urged her to get more from her sister, who was a dressmaker in Paris. She knew I was reasonably well off, but at first she had no idea of my resources. For a year and more we had no car; we walked everywhere and carried our parcels back from Grasse, and then we bought a sturdy Citroën and took on Félicie's husband, Maurice, as a sort of half-time chauffeur, to look after it. During this phase of virtue, Odette felt obliged to write letters to Jane expressing her devotion to me, enquiring intelligently about my health and diet, vowing never to disturb my English ménage. Jane replied in a friendly spirit. There was an exchange of small presents. When we built Lou Pidou, Jane bought and sent her a picture by Nevinson.

I began introducing Odette to various friends of mine who came to Cannes or Nice. I allowed it to appear gradually that I had a much greater freedom financially than I had let her conclude at first. I began to think of her future and arranged for her an independent income.

Now the reader must not suppose that, during what I have called the phase of virtue in Odette, it was always halcyon weather between us. She had her alternations of mood; her bad times when she would quarrel unreasonably about the merest trifles. Every month for a day or so she was deranged. She would scold the servants, and refuse to speak at meals, and she carried on a war of petty insults with our landlady, la Baronne de Rivière, who lived close by. She was carrying on an acrimonious correspondence with a brother-in-law about some money he had borrowed from her, and, all unknown to me, she was writing stinging letters to various people who had stirred her vindictiveness during her adventures in Georgia and Russia. And so soon as other people, and especially people who were new to us, began to come into this life of ours together, she developed a self-conscious excitability of a very formidable sort. If I were to write this story in sufficient detail I could trace with every increment in our spending, with every enlargement of a circle of acquaintance, with every extension of opportunity that opened before her, the gradual return of Odette from her original abjection to a state of unbalanced over-stimulation and egotistical assertion. The luck of capturing me—for she saw me at first through a magnifying mist of prestige and she had felt most desperately poor and unsuccessful—stunned and tranquillized her into good behaviour for a time. Then she began to assert herself. She forgot our original treaty and recalled her discredited ambitions. It was the return to a world of suppressed impulses and banished memories. Refreshed and comforted, Odette resumed her defeated attack on the world and distinction.

From my selfish and concentrated point of view she began to make herself a nuisance to me.

She had, I discovered, no idea of entertaining people except by what schoolgirls call "showing off." When we two were alone together in the Lou Bastidon stage, I was her only audience and I was a very restraining audience. She went carefully with me and her rôle was one of devotion. But with the appearance of new people, I became, so to speak, the actress's protector in the box, and at the new audience I had gathered for her she let loose a repertory of poses that I had hitherto inhibited. She became a noisy exhibitionist. She talked ever more vociferously of her early life in the "embassy," of her deep spiritual life as a nun, of her religious experiences, of her marvellous explorations in the Caucasus and North Africa, in regions hitherto inaccessible to refined women (and why), of the books she had written and the books she was going to write, of her marvellous insight into the psychology of peoples and her distinctive descriptive talent, of her great and wonderful love for me. She would contradict me and shout me down if I tried to deflect the talk to any subject but herself. Then she would stage a quarrel with me and forgive me—with a headlong rush round the table to embrace me. Or she would discourse, with vivid particulars, on the wonders of our sexual intimacy.

I sat it out, with amazement giving place to rage.

When at last the visitors departed out of this storm, I would go off for a walk under the olives to recover my equilibrium and she would retire to her room to sulk and weep because I had not supported her, let her down, tried to snub her. The dinner-time would be devoted to this grievance. "Oh God," I would cry, "*shut* up."

"When I have devoted my life to you!"

Then perhaps another forgiveness and then a long tirade against our departed guests, my friends. The Englishwomen were dowdy and dull; the men had no manners, and so forth and so on. . . .

I would sit like a sulky schoolboy reflecting that there was now only a fortnight (or was it ten days?) left before my return to England.

After dinner we would go off to our respective studies and perhaps I would see no more of her until she came flitting, attractively disrobed and scented with jasmine, into my room to "say good night" and declare and demonstrate her unfaltering devotion to me.

"Why don't you understand me? I do it all for you. I want to be a credit to you."

Despite these storms, these increasing revelations of a fundamental incompatibility between us, I did really get through a great deal of work at Lou Bastidon; the life was extraordinarily healthy there; she had a setting of sunshine, cypresses, blue mountains and the distant sea—and I could for a time dispel my gathering storms of irritation at her increasing aggressiveness, in laughter.

It was always, I reflected, open to me to go away. And at that time I had no one else in my head as a possible alternative to Odette. I was not in the least in love with her, but I went through most of the gestures of love effectively enough. It seemed to me that this was all that life had to offer me. She need occupy no larger a place in my life than I had given her; I need not introduce her to friends who would not like her; and, to make my sense that I was free to go away more real, I set to work transferring money to her and setting up a trust in America that would give her an independent income. But I was so far set upon keeping with her, and so generally satisfied with this intermittent life I led in the Provençal sunshine that presently—being rather weary of the excessive sanitary simplicity and many practical inconveniences of Lou Bastidon—I began building a larger prettier *mas*, with bathrooms and a good kitchen, a garage, visitors' rooms, and so forth, on a very picturesque bit of land with a big mass of rock and torrent and some good trees, a quarter of a mile away. This was Lou Pidou, and it was finished in 1927. I bought a second car; I took on Maurice Goletto, Félicie's husband, as my full-time chauffeur, and I made every preparation for a permanent settlement in Provence. And, concurrently with these commitments, I was making Odette independent by a further settlement in England, settling a usufruct of the house on her, and making it possible for me, if she became intolerable, to walk out of Lou Pidou at any time, and never bother myself seriously with it or her again until the usufruct fell in. I tried to make the situation clear to her, but such an abandonment of property was inconceivable to her Levantine mind. Her confidence in her hold on me grew with every warning and every reconciliation. By the time she was convinced she was indispensable, she had achieved complete impossibility.

I liked building Lou Pidou, and I did many things in the way of flattery to foster her assurance. Entwined in some flourishes over the fireplace I made the builder write "Two Lovers built this House," and it is there to this day, and on some of the windows I wrote *vers libre* about vines and olives and love. All that seemed as good as marriage-lines to Odette.

The resumption of her former self—of her "true self" as the phrase goes—went on apace after the building of that house. The danger of losing me, which had had the most salutary influence on her behaviour in the beginnings of our liaison, seemed to have passed altogether. She began to boast to all comers of *her* house, *her* cars, *her* private income—it amounted to about eight or nine hundred pounds a year but she preferred to call it a thousand—and it came entirely from me. My godlike quality diminished with every freedom I gave her. She was presently making plans for my future as well as her own. she wanted pearls; she wanted a salon in Paris, where I, under her influence, could play a more positive part in the political world. The French political world, be it understood!

She became more and more exasperating. She threw a hard intensity into these silly ambitions. The tension rose at times to the breaking point. And yet, as a Lark, she remained extremely tolerable. And I continued to get a lot of work done down there. . . .

At times she could touch the springs of great fountains of laughter in me.

One day, for instance, we were entertaining Sir Wilfred Grenfell and his wife. They were very anxious to enlist my support for his Labrador missions. They stayed in our little guest-house for two or three days. Odette was very ambitious to be invited to Labrador; to pervade the coast with her talk and personality and perhaps to pursue another of those remarkable "studies" that I suppose the curious, when this is published, will still find available to read; *A Foreigner Visits the British Sudan*, *Au Pays du toison d'or*, *Dans l'Aurès inconnue*, *My Year in Soviet Russia* and *Les Oases dans la montagne*. I warned her very carefully of the limitations of Sir Wilfred and his lady, and for two days nothing was said or done in Lou Pidou that would have been unseemly in an Anglican vicarage. Then one evening I remarked—I realize unwisely: "You will meet a lady at lunch tomorrow, a Mrs. Casenove. She has a little son—the last surviving descendant, it is said, of the great Casanova."

"Casanova!" said Sir Wilfred. "Casanova? Now let me see: what exactly did Casanova *do*?"

I saw a strange brightness in Odette's eye but I was powerless to intervene—I knew what she was going to say.

She told him in a word.

The word, the awful word, the vulgarest and most indecent of English bad words, fell between us. A tremendous silence followed, which I broke at last.

"Casanova," said I, ignoring that explicit word, "wrote some celebrated *Memoirs*."

"Ah yes, the *Memoirs*," said Sir Wilfred, and the thread of conversation was restored.

After a time Odette, who had startled even herself, came back into our polite conversation about memoirs. She supplied information about Madame de Sevigny....

But they did not ask Odette to go to Labrador.

And another cheerful explosion was when Lou Pidou was raided by Mrs. Cecil Hanbury, whose husband owned (for her) those gardens at La Mortola I made the scene of *Meanwhile*. She brought over Sir William Joynson Hicks (afterwards Lord Brentford) and a large retinue and they all sat down to a tumultuous tea. Joynson Hicks was the most prudish of Home Secretaries, but he had an admiration for Mrs. Cecil

Hanbury. He was developing what I may call an elderly responsiveness that sometimes annoyed Lady Hicks. Mrs. Hanbury brought him over to my ménage to be shocked—and he was shocked.

At that time there was much discussion about a novel, a very mild and decorous novel, turning on the theme of homosexuality, *The Well of Loneliness* by Miss Radclyffe Hall. Odette found its suppression very exciting; she made it her standard topic, and she attacked Hicks as the party responsible—he was Home Secretary—with some intensity.

Most of us did not know what was going on; there was a great babble of conversation, and there came one of those general pauses that so often cut abruptly across the artificial noises of entertainment.

"But Jix," she said—she had adopted his newspaper nickname from the moment I introduced her—"I cannot see why there should be more objection to two women going to bed together than a man and a woman. At any rate, whatever they do, they don't run the risk of producing some miserable child."

Joynson Hicks, who was further embarrassed by the presence of a grave, elderly-mannered son who evidently disapproved furiously of the whole occasion, reached his limit with that remark.

"I had rather not discuss the question further," he said....

General conversation was resumed—hectically.

And on another occasion about that time we met the Mathiases and they took us over to lunch with Sir Alfred Mond and Lady Mond at Monte Carlo. Odette was put near Sir Alfred. Two gems of conversation flashed down the table to me.

One was Odette saying, "When you say 'Ve,' Sir Alfred, do you mean 'Ve English' or 'Ve Jews'?"

Then I lost the thread for a time. Then I heard Sir Alfred,

excessively wrath, saying: "In Judea we would have stoned you—and serve you *right*!"

She had raised that little matter of the *Well of Loneliness* again.

It is impossible to dislike a woman who can create such situations altogether. She, and the report of her, did scare off a terrible multitude of tedious genteel people, who might otherwise have descended upon me. But on the other hand she gave way to such storms of colloquial indecency that they were boring and oppressive; the happy indecorums were the rarer ones. When things were plainly going from bad to worse, I would see her long hands gesticulating down the table towards me. "I learnt it all from that man," she would cry. "Every word I know—I got from him."

It was plausible, but untrue. The half-dozen forbidden English words she used as conversational hand-grenades had been acquired by her long before I knew her.

She began to realize more and more that I knew a great number of people who figure in the papers, and that I led a much ampler social life than she had supposed. This marched with her expanding social ambitions. I was acutely aware of the injustice of leaving her alone in France when I returned to a fuller life in England, and since she seemed discontented and inharmonious with the miscellaneous society she was coming to know on the Riviera, we discussed the establishment of a flat in Paris. She was unable to settle down to writing—when I was away. The great book on her convent experience was proving altogether beyond her powers, and the failure of anyone—except the friends to whom she presented copies—to appreciate her sedulously written travel descriptions discouraged her. She had two sisters and a number of other high-voiced ex-pupils of Miss Green; she had a varied collection of acquaintances; she could use me for introductions very usefully, and it seemed quite possible that in Paris she might be able to keep up the excitement of life during my absences.

But while the Parisian project was still in the air, soon after we had taken possession of Lou Pidou, came the devastating telegram from my son Frank which told me that Jane had cancer and could live only six months. I returned to London post-haste and spent those last six months as I have told in *The Book of Catherine Wells*.

After Jane's death I went back to Paris to meet Odette. I did not know what I meant to do with my life. I had always supposed that my wife would survive me, since she was younger than I, and that the broad, happy and dignified life she was leading at Easton Glebe and at Whitehall Court in London would continue to her end. She loved her house and garden; she had, as I have told, a complete control of our finances, and she was always increasing the amenities and beauties of the place. Many people liked her and a good few had reason to love her kindly generosity. I was as much the friendly visitor as the master in these two establishments, and, even up to these last sad and noble months of her life, we had many happy and tranquil days together.

Provence, I realized, with the life I had led there, was a mere escape into sunshine, a change and a refreshment, and no sort of home. Odette, with her incessant voice, her perpetual quarrels with the servants, her incapacity for self-effacement, had prevented the development of any sense of home there. And the idea of bringing her, over-dressed, under-bred, feverishly aggressive, uncontrollable and unteachable, to England was unthinkable. I would not have submitted Grout, my decent gardener, or my pleasant English maids, to her for a moment, for she was a hard exacting mistress. She would have insulted my London secretaries and tried to make them do humiliating odd jobs for her. She would have warped and bent all my friendships out of recognition.

So I told her in Paris that I meant to keep on Easton for myself, and to continue our treaty just as though Jane was alive. She was to leave me England and I was to give her France. Then came her phase of opportunity. Suppose then, when I was sore and sorrowful about Jane, about her death, about the way in which I had permitted our temperamental unfitness to spoil the sentimental completeness of our lives together; suppose then that Odette had achieved any intimations of understanding and tenderness! I did not know then that there was any other possibility of woman's love in the world for me. Adventures perhaps but not close continuing intimacy. Odette had only to be reasonable and mildly loving just at that time to win the confidence I had never given her, and then I might have taken on this fundamentally base and silly woman as my wife. But it needed a little time at least before I could be able to think of any other woman as a wife. Odette gave me no chance. She met me excited and headlong. She proclaimed to me that now I must sell Easton Glebe and set up our flat in Paris and in fact become French, a French *mari*, and, when I told her I had not the slightest intention of either selling that dear house of Jane's or handing it over to her, she burst into recriminations and tears on her own account.

I could plead a good case for Odette against myself. I was the means of inflicting immense disappointment on her. In defence I declare that never did I make love to her as a lover should—with pleading and admiration. I never professed even the intention to be faithful to her. She offered herself to me and I took her upon terms. That was something she was always trying to ignore. She was always trying to treat me as the conquered male—and I was never in the slightest degree conquered by her. Nor was I submerged in any delight at bravery or tenderness in her. She was sensually gratifying and that was the main link between us. She never *got* me—as Rebecca got me—by any reality of mental wealth; at its best her mind was uncreatively critical; and so she was always struggling passionately against the facts when she sought to put things as if I was indeed her lover. She was always struggling to conceal from herself her incredible want of power over me. But from everlasting to everlasting, in all the wide world, no man will ever love such an egotism as Odette.

In 1928–29–30 I was very busy upon *The Science of Life* and *The Work, Wealth and Happiness of Mankind*, and during that time I was, to the best of my ability, working out a *modus vivendi* with her. I wanted to work with her and I wanted to give her a fair deal. I loved my house Lou Pidou, and in her malignant way she ran that quite efficiently. I took a flat in Auteuil and furnished it very agreeably for her. There she acted as hostess to a great diversity of people. But after Jane's death and before the flat was inaugurated, Odette had a misfortune that sent her wildly astray. She contracted an inflammation of the maxillary sinus, and this necessitated first an operation by a Grasse surgeon which was unsuccessful and then another in Paris. This affliction is not only very painful but makes the breath very disagreeable.

Now the standards of behaviour in illness vary very widely in our world. Not only the disposition but the training of people like Jane and the rest of my family turns them towards self-effacement. We all want to get away by ourselves and give as little trouble as possible; do as we are instructed, and get well quickly. We feel apologetic about it. But I have never known Odette apologetic for anything she was or did.

The Levantine habit, with its general bias for dramatic display, makes the most and not the least of an illness. It is an occasion for violent emotion all round. The patient suffers as evidently as possible; is as difficult as possible, and demands incredible feats of propitiation from everyone upon whom she has a claim. And since Odette, after five years of intermittent intimacy with me, was still resolved to impose the rôle of a devoted rich lover upon me, she found my behaviour excessively discordant. I could not feel a spark of distress about this bit of super-dentistry. I had seen Jane face a really painful illness and go on to certain death without flinching, and the fuss Odette made disgusted me. Jane had died, sweet and brave and tired out, holding my hand. Was I to start play-acting over a face-ache in Paris?

I got Odette the best of nurses and surgeons; made all reasonable arrangements for her comfort, and went off to London and Easton to go on with my work until she could be restored to dignity and self-control. There was nothing I could do to help her effectively. The doctors were perfectly willing to administer opiates. But she wanted me to be at hand to scream at; have agonies and fears at; clutch at and astonish with the unparalleled intensity of her feelings, and she wanted to show me off to all her Parisian acquaintances as a marvel of patient solicitude. When I departed, she had to adjust her picture and rave about my callousness and the amazing unrequited love she had borne me and still bore me.

The operation was skilfully performed and quite successful and in her convalescence Odette not only wrote reams of reproaches to me in England, but managed to get a love affair going with her doctor. A doctor to these Latin women is an irresistible temptation. His duties afford openings that they feel it a sin to waste.

I found allusions to the doctor cropping up in her letters. He had blue eyes like me; he was hard and resolute like me; there was a sense of power about him like me. There seemed no limit to Odette's research for resemblances between us. I doubt if there was a limit. I suppose that in her queer mind the nearer he came to being a twin, the less the infidelity.

By this time I was so bored with Odette and her incessant fantastic self-explanations, that I was beginning to work out the possibility of a separation. I thought, if I could establish her in a flat in Paris, I could gradually widen a separation without putting her to open shame for a failure. I thought she could find congenial reactions in Paris. But I wanted to keep hold of my pretty house at Grasse, for I could work well there. I loved the atmosphere of the place very much and had still my very congenial Golettos there. (Odette quarrelled with them and dismissed them later.) At that time I was very much the widower. I had no other woman in view with whom I could think of living; I was not very well—I was in fact becoming diabetic though I did not know this—and I was disposed to regard Odette as still a possible associate, a prostitute-housekeeper, to put it plainly.

We furnished the flat in Auteuil and I became, as it were, the occasional paying-guest. I never pretended to be master there. We entertained, but I do not talk French skilfully—and I was bored by the social life she conducted. So soon as she was fairly convalescent, I took her in my car to Brittany; and, later on, finding her unhappy and mentally ill, I took her for a tour in Switzerland and Geneva, returning at last to Lou Pidou. She had had, as I have said, an affair with her doctor. She gave me unsolicited versions of the trouble—which varied widely. He had spoilt life for her. I doubt if he was much to blame. I refused to be excited into a triangular situation, but I was sorry for her feverish disorder. She had reveries of shooting him—but Odette is not the stuff to shoot. She seems to have gone so far as to get a pistol—I never bothered to take it away from her. I took her to Switzerland and tried to distract her by interesting myself in a densely stupid novel she was projecting, *La Capitulation.*

I wanted to work very badly. I had two very heavy projects which I wished to carry out, *The Science of Life* and *The Work, Wealth and Happiness of Mankind*, and, at that time, I was obsessed by the idea that my strength was failing and that, if I wanted to get things done, I had to do them forthwith. In January Julian Huxley was with us at Lou Pidou, and we worked out the concluding sections of *The Science of Life* together. Then I took up my plans for *The Work, Wealth and Happiness of Mankind.*

In the spring of 1929 in London, I met Antonina Vallentin, who has since married Luchaire—the secretary of the Institute of International Co-operation (until 1931). At that time she was playing the rôle of hostess to gatherings of the liberal Germans who centred upon Stresemann. She was an active able woman; her book on Stresemann is excellent and her *Poet in Exile* (Heine) a classic; and she was the acting secretary of a vigorous society which held meetings in the Reichstag building and invited distinguished people from abroad to address them. She asked me to figure in that select band of lecturers and I went. There were one or two things I wanted to say as publicly as possible. I called my paper "The Common Sense of World Peace" (it is printed in my book *After Democracy*) and by heroic efforts Antonia translated it into German and got it printed in time to distribute at the lecture.

I refused to let Odette come with me on this expedition. Her vociferated judgments on Germany and France and the war would have been an intolerable nuisance. I went alone and met and liked Stresemann, Einstein and a number of other people—and also I met someone else, of much greater importance to me, Moura.

I found a letter in the Eden Hotel in that Russian scrawl of hers. She would be at my lecture if she could get a ticket; she wanted to see me again.

She was waiting for me as the lecture audience dispersed, tall and steady-eyed, shabbily dressed and dignified, and at the sight of her my heart went out to her. "It's Moura!" I said.

"Aige-gee," said she.

"Could you hear?"

"I heard every word, my dear."

"We must meet and talk. Do you remember? The last time

we came out of a meeting together was after the meeting of the Soviet of the North in Leningrad, and everybody was singing the 'Internationale.'"

But I must tell of that later. Suffice it, so far as Odette was concerned, that Moura came to my room next day and that the day after she dined with Harold Nicolson and myself at the Eden and afterwards spent a long evening with me that terminated in her shabby little apartment. From the moment we met we were lovers, as though there had never been any separation between us. She has always had that unquestionable attraction for me, and unless she is the greatest actress in the world I have something of the same un-analysable magic for her.

We made no vows; we made no arrangements for the future; we just took all the time we could liberate in Berlin to be together while my visit there lasted. Nobody but Nicolson knew anything about it. It was our affair.

But this was a fundamental change from the world of Odette Keun. I remembered what it was to be really in love. My stoical acceptance of the domestic life I had made for myself at Lou Pidou and Paris was undermined.

§8

Disentanglement and Expostulation

I was already very tired of Odette in 1928; I rediscovered Moura in 1929, and I did not break completely with Odette and become Moura's open and professed lover until 1933. We were lovers, but in conspiracy. This is a long period of shilly-shally and though it all happened within the past five years—I am writing early in 1935—I find it almost as hard to disentangle the phases of purpose in my conduct as I did the earlier twistings and turnings of my affections between Isabel and Jane when I wrote my main *Autobiography*. It is manifest that in these moods and phases I was never entirely consistent with myself; that I did not perceive clearly what was happening in me, and I suppose that from here onward I am, with the best intentions in the world, unconsciously rationalizing. I not only rationalize but I incline to self-justification. I am nearer to these events and consequently less detached and impartial.

I will try to set down in order the chief masses of motive that seem to me to be responsible for my fluctuations. I think it will be less tedious and clearer to do that than to tell a long, intricate and inevitably inexact story of comings and goings.

The ruling motive system in my life, I believe, the ruling but not always the most powerful system, has been that intellectual and productive process which I may roughly call my life-work. It is certainly the most sustained system. I have dealt with that quite fully in the latter part of the *Experiment in Autobiography*. I have projected it as the life-work of Steele in *The Anatomy of Frustration*, 1936. There is no need to describe it again here but it has to be borne in mind that what this "Postscript" deals with is not the main strand of my life but the sexual, domestic and intimate life sustaining it.

In 1928 because, I think, of some change in my glandular life and, it may be, because the death of Jane had made me more acutely aware of mortality, I was disposed to anxiety; I thought my time was drawing towards its end, and I was fussily urgent to get on with the scheme of work now embodied in *The Science of Life*, *The Work, Wealth and Happiness of Mankind*, *The Shape of Things to Come* and various minor satellite papers, lectures and so forth. I did not want therefore to have any fundamental disruption of my working conditions. The periodic migration to and fro from Lou Pidou to England (I never regarded Auteuil as more than a place of passage) and back worked reasonably well. I could get days and weeks for concentrated planning and writing. Although I knew clearly that I now loved Moura more than I did any other woman, I thought we had come together too late. I wanted to see all I could of her, but I had not the sense of available life and vigour sufficient to disrupt everything and begin again with her. I thought it was better for her—at least I ascribe that much unselfish thought to myself—that she should find a place in life independent of me.

In 1929 she was thirty-six, very attractive and animated, though her dark hair was streaked with grey. I was glad of what she gave me, but I had not then the determination to monopolize her that a really healthy male should have had. I thought she ought to marry well and have a man who would serve and worship her as it seemed to me she deserved. I felt a great tenderness and solicitude for her. The fact that she was manifestly very poor hurt me. Directly I returned to England I settled a small annuity (two hundred pounds a year) on her, love masquerading as pseudo-camaraderie; I thought it quite possible I should never see her again and I thought she was one of those careless people who might easily come upon extreme want; I schemed for some further provision for her in my will and I kept up a correspondence with her and arranged presently to see her when she came to England. There again we were lovers. But I told her plainly that I should keep Odette going at Lou Pidou; that we must not have a child; that I would not exact fidelity from her. All that seems amazingly pedantic and clumsy-minded to me now. I subordinated her not indeed to Odette but to my work and my pose of balanced integrity. I certainly ought to have got that child and we ought to have taken the consequences. I told her I counted our meetings no more than happy accidents—that I held myself to be free—and that she was free.

"Very well, my dear," said Moura. "As you will. If I happen to be faithful to you that is my own affair."

She came down twice to Easton Glebe in 1929 and 1930

before I sold the place in July 1930. In the spring of 1930 I treated Odette to a holiday by herself in Egypt and the Sudan —simply to get her off my mind and conscience and be free to meet Moura in England without the daily reminder of Odette's letters. I came to rely more and more upon the happiness Moura's companionship gave me. Yet I was carrying on the vestiges of other "affairs" and I still hesitated to take the decisive step of a breach with Odette.

All this is queer and indecisive to me now. My motives had got into loose unsystemized packets. Distraction of work and of the bother of my irritating dispute with the Society of Authors; sheer dread of an upset in my routines; some lurking insufficiency in my love for Moura; a want of faith that anything so good as Moura seemed to be could be real; a sub-conscious scepticism; a suppressed criticism of a certain shiftlessness and vagueness in her and, above all, obscure glandular attacks upon my will and vigour—I fling these handfuls of suggestions at the reader and I am as little able as he will be to estimate their relative values.

In 1931 the pressure of work upon me was diminishing. I was pulling *The Work, Wealth and Happiness of Mankind* through to its end. Yet I still felt old and worn out. I felt my energy ebbing. I came to London and consulted Dr. Norman Haire about some perplexing symptoms that bothered me. He too was perplexed for a time, and then he had a flash of perception. "You are diabetic!" He called in the best man he knew, Dr. Robin Lawrence of the Diabetic Clinic of King's College Hospital, and I set myself to learn the diabetic life.

My pancreas, insulin deficiency, becomes a decisive actor in my story. By putting myself under a diabetic discipline—it was never necessary to resort to insulin—my energy and vigour were so restored as to make a new man of me; I began to behave with renewed decision and steadfastness and to see things clearly, unclouded by any morbid preoccupation with mortality. I am inclined to think that, apart from the elimination of excessive sugar from my blood, the constant watchfulness against carbo-hydrate excess imposed upon me had an invigorating effect upon my general conduct. I began to watch my step more carefully and not to take things as they came to me. At any rate, by the spring of 1932, I was beginning to know my own mind about Odette quite definitely, and to draw everything together into a plan to release myself from her.

But at that time I was still not urgent to lock up my life with Moura. I was content to go on being her intermittent lover so long as she loved me. I find it difficult to recall my very fluctuating feelings about her between our meeting and 1933. I did not acquire that sense of owning and belonging which the true lover should have, so that I could set about the business of disentanglement from Odette with deliberation and a considerable amount of consideration for her. I wanted to "set her up" in life, independently of me; to reconstruct my work and life with my flat at Chiltern Court as the centre of operations; to make myself independent of ever-present feminine companionship, and to have Moura coming (and going) at her own sweet will. That was how things were between 1929 and 1932. I was beginning to drop all pretence of wanting Moura to be "free," and my own "freedoms" were becoming more and more theoretical, but there was something so simple and delightful in our intermittent encounters, some vagrant adventurous quality in both of us, that kept us from coming to grips with each other, from going into particulars and being realistic with each other, as we should have to do if we married or set up housekeeping together or had a child.

I kept Odette as ignorant as I could of the existence of Moura. I wanted to settle with Odette without the development of a triangular situation which Odette was bound to make public and vulgar. I find scarcely an intimation of the existence of Moura in my engagement books for these years; I was afraid of Odette's jealous prying eyes; and for the same reason I reduced Moura's correspondence to a minimum. I do not know whether it is evidence of a certain obtuseness in me, or of my profound belief in Moura, that I did not consider the possibility of resentment on her part at this restriction. "France belongs to Odette," I said.

I expected Moura to take that as a reasonable arrangement and, what is still more remarkable, she did. It made our meetings vivid, our time together intense, and I do not think that either of us felt when we parted that we might never meet again. In 1931 Moura was knocked down by a taxi in Berlin and badly scarred on the forehead. She never mentioned it in any letter. "What was the good of worrying you about it?" she said, when I asked her about the scar.

But that scar accused me. And I was growing more and more ashamed to be living on five or six thousand a year, while Moura lived in odd lodgings and wore old and cheap clothes. She took money and presents from me, it is true, but with difficulty. I think it spoilt her picture.

All through 1932 I find indications in my engagement books of her increasing importance in my London life. We went about together more and more openly. We stayed with Lord Beaverbrook at Cherkley for a week-end. I gave her a latchkey to my flat.

This was how things were developing about Odette in 1930–31 and 32. I was resenting her behaviour more and more; I was threatening to leave her and denying that I had any great love for her, but I was telling her nothing about Moura.

Odette's original pose of an intense devotion to me had served its purpose and had evaporated. She was playing the rôle now of the brilliant and beautiful woman with a rich, well-managed and subjugated lover, and she was carrying on with fits of temper, scenes and moodiness, when it was clear that I was indisposed to play this new uncovenanted part. I stayed as little as I could in Paris, where I found her social ambitions and enterprises intolerably boring; and at Lou Pidou, I taught her to play badminton to keep myself exercised; went for walks alone; slipped off to talk to Little e (who had built a villa at Mougins), or Maugham or the friendly Boissevains, and grappled with the difficulties of *The Work, Wealth and Happiness of Mankind.* People came to lunch and we lunched and dined out, but Odette's disposition to show off and make stupendous scenes at table increased. Presently she abandoned the Paris flat—which had cost me a thousand pounds to furnish. She was making no headway and I have an impression she had got into some entanglement, during one of my absences, that spoilt Paris for her and made her uneasy with our servants. At any rate she dismissed two sets of them suddenly with great vehemence, and at her request I gave up the flat before my three years' tenancy was up.

Matters entered upon a new phase when I was discovered to be diabetic in August of 1931. I had kept the fact from her until I found it necessary to break my word to return to her at a certain date. I explained that I was under treatment and that I should need some weeks more; and she came headlong to London. This was a fundamental breach of our treaty. But she had always wanted to come to London; Englishmen, she found, were good credulous listeners, and Englishwomen had low voices that could be overcome with scarcely an effort, and here at last was the door opening.

She dramatized the situation. The rich and well-known lover was to become an invalid and she would come to London, be trained in a hospital and treat him, and devote the rest of her life to his helplessness. Marriage would ensue—marriage with afternoons and evenings off and really brilliant social displays. It was a glorious dream. She wrote to Amber to tell her of the romantic surprise she had in store for me and also to Norman Haire, who had dined with us in Paris. She demanded the addresses of hotels and suchlike information. Amber warned me at once by telephone, and so I rang up Norman Haire, who I guessed would also be privy to the raid and lured him into a betrayal, for which he was subsequently punished by a series of insulting letters. And Amber was never suspected. Duly appraised, I did my best to stop Odette at the eleventh hour. "Damn you! Keep out of London, anyhow," I telephoned, ignoring my rôle of the ailing Tristan waiting for Isolde.

I would not have her in my flat except for one coldly polite dinner to meet some friends who had visited us down there; and I explained with the utmost brutality that the sooner she went back to France the better. But she held on gallantly to her conception of the situation. She went through a parade of being trained to nurse a diabetic case at King's College Clinic, though Lawrence and everyone told her that I was quite able to look after myself. It was the August Bank Holiday season; nearly everybody she had met in France was out of town, and I succeeded in returning her to her proper territory within a week. I induced her to go by promising to join her later; I had a great mass of work upon the proofs of *The Work, Wealth and Happiness of Mankind* to do, which it was impossible to tackle in London in August, and I went myself to Lou Pidou at the end of August and stayed there with her for some weeks, working, playing badminton with John Wells the painter and the Boissevains, and discussing the situation.

I had always felt that I should dislike Odette in London, but I did not realize how ashamed I could be of her until I saw (and heard) her against a London background. She was disagreeable, noisy, aggressive and over-dressed enough in Paris, but the grey quietness of London's abundance made her altogether intolerable. In the flaming Provençal scene, and particularly at home in Lou Bastidon or Lou Pidou, rushing about the garden, scolding the gardener, scolding the servants, scolding the workmen, gossiping with the neighbours, attending to the obsequious pet dogs she found necessary to existence, keeping the house vehemently spick and span, as she did, being taken for a treat and excited shopping to Nice, going for long walks with me, and existing generally in the open air, she was a different person altogether from her vain assertive city self.

And I too perhaps was a different person down there. I had a formula for making love to her there; we had common interests in my rock, with its ilex trees and wild flowers, in our oil-jars and irises, in our new rose-garden, our agaves, our oranges, the alterations we were always making to the house, and we had a tradition from our first successful year or so at Lou Bastidon, to which we could revert. (See *The World of William Clissold, passim.*)

Another thing that enabled us to get along at Lou Pidou was that there I was her only audience. Consequently she played to me to be effective to me, and she was coming to understand the sort of effects I would tolerate. But directly other people came along her devotion to me gave place to some other rôle to which, as often as not, I was the villain antagonist. After the temporary audience departed, she would fall into attempts to justify her conduct. Or she would sulk and avoid me. She was tremendously wounded by her London repulse, but she had the sense to make an effort to save the situation. I returned to London before my birthday in September because, through an odd lapse from my customary disregard of anniversaries, I wanted to spend it, as I had spent the two previous ones, with Moura, and then at the end of the month I sailed for America to see *The Work, Wealth and Happiness of Mankind* through the press and try and estimate what the great slump meant there. England was just going off the Gold Standard and economically it was a very exciting time.

While I was in America Odette dismantled the Paris flat and brought down the furniture to a farmhouse adjacent to Lou Pidou which I had acquired from the Golettos. So far was I from intending to give up the place at that time. After doing that Odette was seized with a fit of restlessness and went off for a trip to Morocco.

I returned to Cannes by an Italian boat at the end of November (1931) and now my energies were reviving and I was full of schemes of work. I wrote what I think are three good books before the end of 1932, *The Shape of Things to Come*, *The Autocracy of Mr. Parham*, and *The Bulpington of Blup*, and I did a fair amount of minor writing. I went to Madrid in May 1932 to give a public lecture and see the new Government. I would not take Odette on this expedition, but afterwards I relented by telegram and she brought the car and chauffeur with her to Barcelona. Thence we had a good tour in Spain—our last holiday together. We quarrelled, but not excessively, because now I did not care enough for her to contradict her, and she was beginning to have an inkling of her slipping hold upon me. We came back via Madrid and lunched with the Bibescos (Prince Bibesco was the Roumanian ambassador and his wife was Elizabeth Asquith) and there Odette had one of her lapses into noisy exaltation and talked so outrageously that the governess suddenly swept herself and Elizabeth's daughter out of the room. "That may be the last time you inflict that sort of disgrace upon me," I said, and I sent her home by train from Barcelona, driving the car myself by road.

We tried to get to a *modus vivendi*. All the time she was professing, and I think feeling, an extravagant love for me—but it was plainly an intense exhibitionist possessiveness blended with an eager physical passion. She would never give me up—she would die—and so on. She would commit suicide. I allowed myself to be displayed and talked at with a deepening discomfort. But I made it clear to her that my English and American worlds were my own to do as I pleased in; that for me she had no meaning now outside Lou Pidou; and, moreover, quite apart from the possibility of my going away, since I was now a man of sixty-five and she was twenty years younger, it was best she should develop other interests in life. She was always going to be left to herself part of the time; she could count on that, and presently I should die and she would be left altogether.

I wanted her to write her convent novel and develop and exploit her disposition for descriptive and critical articles, but she would not hear of that. Her Catholicism had given her the idea of Good Works as an outlet for a noble woman; her experiences in Algiers had taught her that the further a civilized woman is from normal civilization, the more interesting she becomes; and so she proposed to go into training in Switzerland as a nurse with a view, a very distant view of which she began to talk more and more abundantly, to a philanthropic mission in darkest Africa. She has been playing at this training ever since, and writing importantly about her expedition to various Colonial Offices. She has now, I believe, transferred the objective to South America. She will, I know, die in the course of that training, however long she lives, with her philanthropic purpose completely unachieved. However I fell in very heartily with these ideas; she installed herself in Geneva in July, and I returned to London, greatly relieved. I spent July and most of August in England, returned to Geneva and picked her up there in late August and drove her over the Col de Galibier to Grasse (to the public shame of Maurice Goletto my engine boiled out on that pass, and we had to pack the radiator with snow), and I took her back as far as Aix on her way to Geneva in September, where she stayed until late November.

I went to Lou Pidou at the end of November 1932 and stayed there until March 4th, 1933. It was the last winter I spent in that house. Odette was not enjoying the disciplines of her hospital training, and she had been thinking over our relations, and realizing something of the slow untwisting of the threads that held me. She had looked up the dates of my comings and goings, and I was coming later and going sooner each winter. But she did not take this as a warning symptom; she made it a grievance. She felt her hold slipping and could not realize it was anyone's fault but mine. I was altering in my manner to her, I was avoiding endearments and particularly public endearments, and I was refusing to quarrel with her—her instinct told her to distrust a lover who becomes polite. In the past—it was one of her boasts—she had so provoked me that I had hit her. What was I up to? Moreover she wanted now to come to London so much that it was becoming an obsession. She developed a baseless legend that I had wanted to marry her after the death of Jane and that she had generously left me free.

I thought over this London hunger. "It's not fair to keep you out of London," I said. "But I keep *my* London. If you come to London, you do it on your own behalf; you go about without me, we won't meet, you will never come near my flat. You shall have your friends and I mine. And I warn you—it will probably be the end."

"You'll have to come here for the winters."

"Even that is not inevitable."

"I shall come to London."

I had given her a usufruct of Lou Pidou for life and she had gifts or settlements from me that ensured her between £800 and £1,000 a year, so that I felt no compunction about leaving her. It would be merely a personal detachment and no sort of desertion. And now, arising out of her apprehension of this increasing detachment on my part, she became searchingly jealous. She felt she was being compared with my English women friends; that I saw her at a disadvantage all day while those I met socially were prepared for the occasion. There must be a mistress or mistresses in London and she was being undermined. But who was the woman? She had ineffective dreams of vitriol and pistols and an urgent craving to write a tremendous letter, a series of letters to all and sundry, to and about some person or persons unknown. I had always suspected her of tampering with my correspondence and, though I never pretended to be faithful to her outside of France, she was perpetually asking everyone who came near her from England about my movements and my associations.

There were in London several interesting women with whom I was closely friendly. Every woman does not want to be pressed to make love, but most women like just that much approach from a man that puts him in the relation of a potential lover. There are kisses and endearments, advances and regretful recoils, confidences and small concessions. It is friendship—that can be sincere enough—and an insincerity of love-making that skirts the dangerous edge of becoming sincere. I have had for years a particularly intimate relationship of this sort with Christabel McLaren, who is now Lady Aberconway. We met when she was a brilliant young hostess in the days when Elizabeth von Arnim ruled, and before I had ever set eyes on Moura; we talked and our talk was gleeful; we conceived a fondness for each other that has waxed and sometimes waned for years. We have been on our guard against jealousy and that, I suppose, seeing that neither of us is pedantically virtuous, is why we have kept out of each other's arms. She is far too embedded in her world, with household, children and a position, ever to become mine in any full sense of the word, and there is nothing much to appeal to us in an afternoon of adultery. That would be too much and not enough for either of us. We tell each other our troubles very faithfully and find it helpful at times to see things through each other's sympathetic eyes. And we write to each other gaily and unrestrainedly. The fact that we have never been lovers we call our "guilty secret." Few of our intimates suspect it.

So Odette, hovering suspiciously over my mail while I was away in the town of Grasse, found an envelope with a coronet irresistible and opened it, to discover a letter beginning "Darling" and going on to discuss why it was that each of us, being the most meritorious of creatures, found our beds in life were made almost entirely of crumpled rose leaves. Whereupon Odette exploded and gave me just the occasion I needed to break with her, without dragging Moura into a vociferous public dispute. There were great scenes. She would make copies of that scandalous letter; she would publish it to all the world; she would send it to McLaren. I knew well enough that she could publish nothing and do no mischief worth talking about between the McLarens. I listened to her with an exasperating calm, for my mind was made up—seemed to me to have been always made up. "If you open my letters," I said, "I will come here no more," and my long-suspended resolution to end things with her dropped like a portcullis between us.

It is remarkable with what swiftness outworn ties can dissolve at last. I went back to England and then returned to pack my more personal belongings in Lou Pidou. Odette saw me come and go, incredulous at my detachment. At the end of May I said goodbye to her for the last time, and behind her farewells it was evident that she thought it was all just another quarrel in an endless succession of quarrels and that I should come back—not so much to her as to our life at Lou Pidou. I tell of my departure from Lou Pidou in the *Autobiography*. I went across Italy to Ragusa, to preside at the Congress of the P.E.N. Club. Thence I went by train to Salzburg where Moura was to meet me.

Odette made for London. Since she insisted on coming, I paid her bill at the Berkeley for a month and left her free to see and entertain her friends and explore London as she chose. It was a sort of parting tip to her—which, after her ungracious fashion, she took not as a gift but as a right. When I returned from Austria she was still holding out beyond the bargain. Some of her friends I did not know; they were journalists, publishers' managers and so forth, or friends of her two English brothers-in-law, or casual acquaintances she had picked up in Egypt and North America; others were people, like Lady Rhondda and her satellites, or St. John Ervine and his wife, of no vital importance in my life, to whom I had introduced her.

I took her to lunch at the Zoological Gardens one day to discuss some details of our future arrangements. It was a monologue, with neglected masculine footnotes, rather than a discussion. She explained our relations from her point of view, talked of a book she was writing, *I Discover the English*, descanted on the marvellous "success" she was having in London, the new friends she was making, the philanthropic expedition she was planning, she proposed to take a motor-car with medicines into Central Africa, and so forth. Under the auspices of my friend Sir James Currie she had got officials in the Colonial Office to take her reverie quite seriously. She was dramatizing herself to them as a woman in a position to equip such a mission. I cast no doubts on these assertions and anticipations. The more she wrapped herself in her fantasy of the brilliant and formidable woman writer, observer and explorer with a streak of philanthropic purpose, the better it was for both of us. She was quite incurious about me. She was too busy spreading her self-protective legend before my dazzled eyes. The tone of that meeting was on the whole quite friendly, and when I returned her duly to the Berkeley she invited me, with a sudden ardour, up to her room. But I did not go up to her room.

Things, however, did not remain at this level. She returned to France and to her Swiss hospital training. For a time she continued to write to me, reciting her lively doings—including the seduction of one of the hospital staff who, like that doctor in Paris, had, it seemed, a quite flattering resemblance to me. It was a rather varied and inconsistent self-portrait, of brilliance, charm and enterprise, she was building up. She was still puzzled by my failure to realize what I had lost in her. But gradually the tune changed and her bitter resentment at my withdrawal from her personal drama came to the surface.

She was going tumultuously through a London in which she heard of me but never saw me, in which I was not only invisible but deaf and blind to her.

I was not reacting to her. I was going about my own affairs with an exasperating disregard of her. But she was not disregarding me. She felt under a necessity to scream at me; to libel, to expose, to hurl missiles, to worry me and hurt me; above all, to be in scenes and encounters face to face with me. She made up a story that I had left her with the usufruct of an impossibly expensive house on her hands and that she had to maintain it out of her own money (which she failed to explain I had given her). She worked up a sense of unfair usage until she believed in it and she persuaded my more credulous friends to write me letters of remonstrance. Various wily women, Lady Rhondda for one, the proprietor of *Time and Tide*, set themselves to champion this ill-used defrauded woman. Ettie Rout, the Eden Pauls, Stella Cobden-Sanderson, John Wells, the portrait painter, were invoked. I told them with varying politeness according to the individual need to mind their own business. Her demands shocked my dear old lawyer, Jules Rainaud, in Grasse, beyond measure; he knew the particulars of our relations, and he wrote to me imploring me not to let her have any more money or countenance her in any way. She had no sense of elementary fair-dealing, and the more I considered her, the more she would persevere. But she was mercenary and a restriction of supplies would bring her to heel.

She had some hundreds of letters from me—mostly intimate and generally indecent as most sexual love-letters must be—and these she threatened to sell. I gave her free permission to sell and assured her that I had no shame about them except a certain shame that I had ever sent love-letters to her.

She began to talk of writing a book that was to reveal my inmost self. I told her to hurry up, because I was doing my *Autobiography* and did not propose to leave much intimate self unrevealed. She had a queer blackmailing impulse in her, and could not imagine that I did not care a rap who knew that I had gone to bed with her or what particulars of our endearments she cared to publish. If she chose to write what she had done and what had been done by her, I could only shrug my shoulders. I had not the slightest shame about them. It was not for me to talk, but if the lady insisted. . . .

Presently Lady Rhondda published a series of articles in *Time and Tide* by her, "H. G. Wells, the Player," and very silly articles they were. Possibly the Editor had had to take the spice of personal revelation out of them. Then I gather they were hawked about among various minor publishers with the spice restored, but Lane and Cape had both had to pay for previous libels by Odette and the proposition did not attract anyone, and the spice became the secret joy of Lady Rhondda and her intimates and a few publishers' readers under-exercised in cheerful normality.

My last meeting with Odette in London was in a restaurant, the Queen's, at Sloane Square. We sat down to lunch together and she recited, as if from a well-considered statement, her conception of the situation. She never paused for anything I had to say.

She named her terms for not selling my letters. But I was

entirely indifferent who owned those scraps of bedding, those intimations of appetite. I was equally disinclined to buy off that terrible book. "All London" would laugh at me when it was published. I said I would take the risk. "Go ahead with it. Be sure to get your money from the publisher in advance, and then I will get *my* damages from him and also, my dear, from the trusts and property I have settled on you. Don't you see that I don't *want* to hurt you, but that you keep on asking me to do so, and that you are anything but immune from punishment."

She tried to develop some bargain about the house by which I should leave it in her hands just as it was and pay a considerable additional annuity to her. "You have enough," I said. "You can write amusingly. You could earn another thousand a year if you chose to work. Ultimately you will. The best thing I have ever done to you is to leave you. When you have got through with all this rage and disappointment, you will see that—though you will never confess to it—I have given you a fair deal."

Then suddenly she left me and went upstairs to the Ladies' Room and was violently sick. She returned presently, refreshed and bright. Her physical elasticity has always been amazing. I took her back in a taxi to her lodging in Tite Street, and in the cab this poor muddle of passion and greeds and desires fell upon me and kissed me and asked me to come in to her there.

"My dear," I said, "you are like a child. You *are* a child—a nasty child. You cannot understand that when you break a thing it is broken and when you kill it, it is dead."

The next time I heard her voice was somewhen in the autumn of 1934. It was about two o'clock in the morning, when the bell of my private telephone woke me up and I took it down to hear her.

"I can't sleep, Pidoukaki; I can't sleep. I'm over-excited and I can't sleep. Have you seen my book?" (This was *I*

Discover the English.) "It's *such* a success. All London is talking of it. It is—everywhere. I've been to a party, such a great party, scores of tables, and Mr. Lloyd George was there and Mr. Baldwin."

"I'm glad you're having a good time, my dear. That's fine. Go ahead with it."

"Why are you so wicked to me, Pidoukaki? I talked about you, I talked *brilliantly*—all the evening."

"Well, well," said I.

"But I said dreadful things about you—dreadful things. I kept them all listening. About you and about your Moura. Do you know I've invented a name for her. It will be all over London. Such a funny name. All London will laugh at you. I call her, not Budberg but Bedbug, the Baroness Bedbug, I. . . ."

I put down the telephone receiver, reflected for a while on something amusingly irresponsible in Odette; assured myself that I had done all I could for her; gave myself complete absolution on her account, and turned over and went very peacefully to sleep.

Then for a time our relations became deliberately indirect. I heard about her from various friends we have in common, and Jules Rainaud of Grasse keeps me posted about her conflicting intentions about my house. Long ago I began paying her sister Maggie, who is a plucky little widow in Paris with three children, a thousand francs a month. I saw no reason for punishing Maggie because I was breaking with Odette; and so that pension and correspondence still go on. Maggie has a queer warm affection for me and sends me intermittent letters telling me of the progress of her children and abusing her sister for her folly in letting me go. (But in fairness to Odette, it has to be recognized that things were not quite so simple as that.)

In the winter of 1934–35 I started to fly to Palermo with Moura for a three-week holiday. But we learnt at Marseilles that the aerodrome at Ostia was flooded, and since we were both too tired to face the long railway journey, we stopped off on the Riviera. We stayed in Mentone and Nice; we visited Somerset Maugham for a week at his Villa Mauresque on Cap Ferrat, and Little e, at her house at Mougins Sartoux. One day Maugham, with an unusually distressful expression on his habitually distressful face, stammered to me, "I've had a letter from Odette."

"A stinker?"

"That—that describes it exactly."

"I've had some hundreds. I hope you don't mind. I don't know how I can stop them."

"I shall write and tell her exactly what I think of her."

"You'll be cross all day if you do. You'll want to rewrite your letter as soon as you have posted it. The best and easiest way to tell her exactly what you think of her is—silence."

But in the end he wrote a brief dignified letter and if she wrote to him again I did not hear of it.

Little e, when her "stinker" came, did not answer it at all.

So Odette is receding out of my life down a *diminuendo* of parting shots. She becomes more and more a crazy self-protective artificiality. Occasionally she writes me descriptions of my cat and my swallows and the nightingales and frogs and roses and fire-flies of Lou Pidou. Charming things they are to have lost, no doubt, but there are plenty of other delights in the world. This, I suppose, is to arouse regret and envy. There are outbursts of epistolary affection in these letters as well as outbursts of wild abuse. I have very little resentment against her and not a scrap of affection for her. She gave me some intensely disagreeable moments, but she never did me any injury worth lamenting, and at her best she was fantastically lively and entertaining. Her good hard limited "Latin" mind, when it was brought to bear on my typescripts and proofs, could produce, not so much criticisms, as warnings of possible misinterpretations that were very often of great value to me. Many of my statements she made me harden and condense. Odette had a mind with some very good points. I think if I had loved her more or had a greater, more enveloping mind, I might have done better for her and by her. But I am not that much a divinity. There is something repulsive in her egotistical vanity that forbids any enduring closeness. There is no "getting on" with Odette, none at all. There is no helping her except upon her own impossible terms. Even when she is sane she is blindly egotistical, a torrent of assertion, pretension and aggression and sooner or later the malignant nerve-storm breaks upon her loyalest ally. R.I.P.

§9
Moura, the Very Human

I do not think that, from the time of my very primitive and boyish sensuous and instinctive passion for Amber, until my wife died in 1927, I was ever, except in the most transitory way, really "in love" with any other woman. I loved and trusted Jane steadily and surely. But my other "love affairs" had much the same place in my life that fly-fishing or golfing has in the life of many busy men. They were all subsidiary to my politico-social interests and my literary work. They were mixed up with my disposition to change the scene and with housekeeping abroad—and they kept me alive and fresh and saved me from humdrum. I was always *near* loving Rebecca during our liaison, as she was often very near loving me, and I did my best to acquire an emotional attitude to the vehement caresses of Odette. After my breach with Rebecca I made a real attempt, as I have told, to adjust myself to Odette—and get on with my proper work. But from 1920 onward there was another presence in my imagination, sometimes remote, sometimes near, and at last coming very near. Her I loved naturally and necessarily and—for all the faults and trouble I shall tell about—she has satisfied my craving for material intimacy more completely than any other human being. I still "belong" so much to her that I cannot really get away from her. I love her still.

I do not think that there is any element of self-deception in my recognition that Moura is outstandingly charming. Quite an exceptional number of people love and adore her, admire her and are urgent to please and serve her. And yet it is very hard to convey the qualities that do make up her commanding distinction. She is a manifestly untidy woman with a scarred and troubled forehead and a broken nose; she is three and forty (1934), with streaks of grey in her dark hair; she is a little inclined to be heavy physically; she eats very fast, taking enormous mouthfuls; she drinks a great deal of vodka and brandy without any manifest results, and she has a broad soft voice flattened perhaps by excessive cigarette-smoking. Generally she is clinging to a distended old black bag which is rarely fastened up properly. She clings to it with very nicely shaped hands which are never gloved and often grubby. Yet I have rarely seen her in any room with other women in which she was not plainly—not merely in my eyes but to many others—the most attractive and interesting presence. Women fall in love with her at sight and men are compelled to come and ask about her and talk about her, with a certain insincere disinterestedness.

I think it is a certain bravery of bearing that first takes people; the fine carriage of her head and the quiet assurance of her pose. Her hair, which comes most effectively to a point in the middle of her broad forehead, has a natural fine-flowing backward wave. Her hazel eyes are always steady and tranquil, her broad Tartar cheekbones give her an expression of amiable serenity, even when she is really in a thoroughly bad temper, and the very negligence of her costume reveals her strong stout shapely body. Any *décolletage* shows a clear fine skin. We both have exceptionally smooth skins. I have never seen her under any circumstances—and I have seen her under some trying ones— lacking in self possession.

I have tried to get something of her physical charm on record, but it defies the camera. I have never known anyone to whom the camera was so hostile, except my daughter-in-law, Marjorie. Photography gets hardly anything of Moura; something of her jolly bearing in a full-length snapshot and something of a curious infantine charm about her downcast face in repose. Usually the camera produces plain ugliness; the face of a savage woman with broad nostrils under a squat nose that was broken in her childhood. She is extraordinarily like the portraits of her ancestor, Peter the Great. I once commissioned Roger Fry to paint her in the hope that he would catch something of that Mouresqueness that makes Moura Moura. He undertook the task with zest; he found her, he declared, the most charming sitter he had ever painted; and he produced the portrait of an ungainly woman staring disagreeably at fate. Sitting to him bored her, and that fact was the only fact about her he rendered faithfully. I gave away that portrait hastily to one of her women friends, who tried it for a few days in her dining-room and then banished it to an attic, face to the wall.

We were in the same room in 1914, at a dinner-party in Petersburg—she remembers it but I do not—but I really met her effectively in Gorky's flat in Petersburg in 1920. She was wearing an old khaki British army waterproof and a shabby black dress; her only hat was some twisted-up piece of black—a stocking, I think—and yet she had magnificence. She stuck her hands in the pockets of her waterproof, and seemed not simply to brave the world but disposed to order it about. She was twenty-seven then; she had seen life in the diplomatic world of Petersburg and Berlin; one husband, Engelhardt, she had divorced; a second husband, Benckendorf, had been murdered by a peasant in Estonia; she had had that fantastic love affair with Bruce Lockhart he recounted in his *Memoirs of a British Agent* and *Retreat from Glory*; she had attempted to escape to get to her children at Tallinn, spent six months in prison and been sentenced to be shot. Then she was paroled. She was now my official interpreter. And she presented herself to my eyes as gallant, unbroken and adorable. I fell in love with her, made love to her, and one night at my entreaty she flitted noiselessly through the crowded apartments in Gorky's flat to my embraces. I believed she loved me and I believed every word she said to me. No other woman has ever had that much effectiveness for me.

Equally difficult is it to record her mentally and morally, though I am doing what I can in the matter. I have found her out in petty deceptions and also in fairly sustained insincerities. Many of them seem motiveless to me. She does not cheat deliberately. It is just her easy way with fact. She likes to stand well with people. She dramatizes herself for this situation or person and that without any sustaining consistency; she is still in many ways like an imaginative child in the early teens. Like a child she believes a thing as she says it; and she is indignant, extremely indignant, at disbelief. I do not now believe a single statement she makes without extensive tacit qualifications. She lies, and also she is carelessly self-indulgent. That I have only realized in the last year or so. She can drink quite enormous quantities of vodka, brandy or champagne without any apparent disorganization. The other night we dined at the Melchetts' and Lord Mottistone, noticing that her glass was refilled with some frequency, declared he would not be beaten by a woman and drank glass for glass with her—with the result that he became a thick-voiced talkative bore, while a quite unruffled soft-voiced Moura sat among the ladies.

Her manners, her bearing, her complexion remain unruffled however much she has had, and it is only as I have watched her and thought her over, that I have come to realize the subtle release from self-criticism, the false reassurance, that alcohol gives her. Alcohol just slightly disconnects her. It frees her from self-consciousness and consistency and it betrays her in no other way. It assures her that everything is all right with her and that she need not bother. And she does not bother.

Mentally she has no great power or originality, but her mind is very active, full and shrewdly penetrating. It is silk, not steel. She thinks like a Russian; copiously, windingly and with that flavour of philosophical pretentiousness of Russian discourse, beginning nowhere in particular and emerging at a foregone conclusion. I say she thinks like a Russian because I suspect that there is some weakness in the very structure of the Russian language and in the tradition of Russian literature that gives those who use it this disposition. She is a cultivated person who thinks after the manner of literary criticism and not along scientific lines. Powerful strands of childish romanticism and deliberate and cherished wilfulness seem essential to the Russian make-up. It is natural that she should resent Tchekhov's tales of Russia and Gerhardi's *Futility*, because the former are criticisms and the latter a caricature of her mental atmosphere. Odette had a far greater lucidity and more penetration, but within the blinkers of a Latin training. Jane and Amber and my daughter-in-law Marjorie had an order in their minds and a conscientiousness in statement and interpretation beyond anything Moura displays. Jane, Amber, Marjorie and my daughter have had science in their education and they think in English forms. Reasons self-direction has got into their blood. In Moura there is no trace of anything of the sort. She is more purely a creature of impulse than anyone I have ever known. Yet she has streaks of extraordinary wisdom. She will illuminate a question suddenly like a burst of sunshine on a wet February day. And, if she is a creature of impulses, the whole quality of her impulses is fine and generous.

In Petersburg in 1920 she did all she could to explain the Russian situation to me and to give me her point of view; and she advised me very helpfully and loyally in a matter where I might have exposed myself to considerable misrepresentation. It was then a practice of the Bolsheviks to invite any prominent foreign visitor to see the Leningrad Soviet in session. Then suddenly he would be announced to the gathering in a eulogistic speech and asked to say something. It was difficult in the circumstances not to respond with hopes and compliments. These were immediately translated into a reckless panegyric of Marxist Communism, published in *Pravda* and elsewhere and telegraphed to Europe, where one arrived later in vain pursuit of the reported conversation. Moura advised me to write my speech beforehand and read it, and further she translated it into Russian. I read it, and when Zorin rose to paraphrase what I had said into the usual glorification of the new régime, I passed him her translation. "That is what I said; read that," and Zorin could do nothing else on the spur of the moment. So Moura saved me from being labelled a red convert, and that I thought a very courageous thing for a woman already suspect to do.

She came to the train on Petersburg station. "God bless you," we said to each other and "I will never forget you." There was a broken sixpence so to speak in each of our brains. Like so many of those broken sixpences in people's lives, it was not always in evidence and yet it was always there.

I have told already of our fragmentary correspondence. In those days letters to Russia went astray and it was unwise to put even personal secrets into letters. We did not see each other for eight years or more and then suddenly those old memories of a whisper in the darkness and eager searching hands flared to bright life again in the foyer of the Reichstag.

"It is *you.*"

I have always, I think, been a little too prone to respect what I conceive to be my obligations. I was under the inertia of my relationship to Odette in 1929, just as I had been under the inertia of my relationship to Rebecca in 1920. I had *had* to be in Grasse at a certain date and hour in 1929, just as I had *had* to be in London in 1920. And that I think is the main reason I left Moura behind me in Berlin. And why I did not go back to Lou Pidou and, in the Russian phrase, "liquidate" the situation with Odette there and then. I think it would have stormed Moura's imagination if I had come back to her imperatively for good and keeps that spring. I wasted four years about it, and instead sent her that miserable little annuity.

I cannot now get the facts of our relationship during 1929 and 1930 into an orderly sequence. I am taking great risks of rearrangement and falsification here and I do not know how they can be avoided. Moura had been kept out of England by some passport difficulty before 1929. Then the barrier, whatever it was—I think it was a personal objection to her on the part of Joynson Hicks, the Home Secretary, on account of some version of the Lockhart story—broke down, and since that time she has come to England and stayed in England as much as she wanted to, subject to the usual alien regulations. And we are constantly together as much as we can be, seeing that we are not married.

But I think it was not merely my ties and habits that prevented my attempting an immediate coalescence of our lives. I think from the outset I had a very clear feeling that there was much about Moura that I had better not know. I did not want to hear her history or know what alien memories or strands of feeling her past had woven into her brain. There was the great Lockhart romance behind her and I thought and think Lockhart a contemptible little bounder. She had married Budberg in Estonia when she came out of Russia and after we had been lovers, and I did not care to imagine the particulars of that marriage. She had a German divorce from him; he had been a hopeless gambler, he had done something shady and he had got away to Brazil. But sometimes he still wrote to her. I thought, and most people who know her think, that when she went to Sorrento to be secretary and keep house for Gorky, she was Gorky's mistress. I knew the dull elaborate vanity and complexity of Gorky's mind, and I cannot imagine he would have left her alone. But she has always denied that there was a sexual relationship between them. Yet he kept a cast of her hand on his writing-table. He flattered her greatly. She corresponded with him—of that I will presently tell more. And he trusted her and looked to her—so that when he was dying he wanted her to be with him.

She told me that altogether she had had six lovers and had never given herself to any other man; Engelhardt, Benckendorf, Lockhart, Budberg, an Italian lover in Sorrento and myself. She is not a feverish lascivious woman like Odette; she has no sensuous initiative, but she loves to be made love to and she is responsive. She told me she found the thought of self-abandonment to anyone with whom she was not in love unnatural and intolerable. There was no need for her to tell me this—she did so somewhen in 1933—but I was only too eager to believe her then. And I believe it now. But that was not my earlier persuasion. I judged her by myself. I thought she had had as many experiences as I, and that they might very well be going on. I pressed her with no questions in those days. She was open and friendly to all comers and I saw no reason then to suspect her of an extreme physical fastidiousness. But she has an emotional fastidiousness and a sentimental integrity. I am sure she was never mercenary, but I saw nothing in her to suppose she was not free and kind. Many women of her lovely quality—Ellen Terry, for example—have been free and kind.

But because I thought like that about her, it was easier for me to accept this irregular liaison in all its irregularity; to suppose we were both in this discursive phase; to go on when she was abroad with those three or four convenient sensuous friendships I had with women in London, and to delay my breach with Odette. Then, if Moura flitted away from me, as she had once flitted towards me, it would be a tolerable disaster. In all these things I think I misunderstood her.

All through those years of delay I was slipping away from this deliberately careless attitude towards a complete fixation of my affections upon Moura. We were drawing closer to each other and she was becoming more and more necessary to me. Or perhaps I was only discovering my real reaction to her quality. She began to haunt me when she was away from me so that I longed to come upon her round street corners in impossible places. One day, in breach of my treaty with Odette and when Moura was away in Germany, I went to an address she had once given me in Paris because of a vague craving that somehow she might be there (it was an hotel and they knew nothing of her), and I was extremely friendly and attentive to a neighbour of mine at Lou Pidou, a Russian woman of between fifty and sixty, simply because she was tall and had an accent like Moura's, saying "*e*ngry" and "*e*nimals" and using "that" for "this" in the same way.

It is quite impossible to measure how much I was being repelled by Odette and how much I was being attracted by Moura in those transitional days, but I think that the magnetism of Moura was by far the greater force. By the end of 1932, I was prepared to do anything and overlook anything to make Moura altogether mine.

We went away for some days in April 1932 to Fothergill's Hotel at Ascot and then I began to talk to her of marriage.

"Let us go on as we are," said she.

"But why?"

It was then we arranged to meet in Austria after the P.E.N. Congress at Ragusa. "And then we must meet for good," said I.

In the evenings Fothergill, dressed in the suit of bottle-green livery cloth, with brass buttons and buckled shoes, would come and talk about food and drink and innkeeping and Russia and the gift of languages to the Baroness and myself. He was a fantastic inn keeper who has written a book about himself, and the pleasure of our stay with him was much enhanced by the fact that three elephants also were among his guests. They were circus elephants out of an engagement; they occupied some of his limitless (Ascot) stabling; they exercised every day in his field and when we went out to see them they would come scampering, trunks up towards us, for the apples they knew we were bringing them. "She's taken an epple out of my pocket," cried Moura, radiant with delight.

We were very happy in Salzburg and Vienna; we went to the green country about Edlach and we went up to the Rax Alp. "This is only the beginning of our life together," I said. "In a little while we will marry."

"But why *marry*?" asked Moura.

We began to dispute about marriage. "I will come to you anywhere," she said.

"But why go away?" said I.

"I'd be a bore if you had me always."

But at Salzburg something was going on that I did not scrutinize. I had not begun to scrutinize Moura. She was sending telegrams to Russia, and she was bothered about something. She told me, for at that time she too was not very defensive against me, that Gorky was anxious to see her. He was very ill, perhaps dying, and he was very anxious to see her. He had lost his son and was lonely. He wanted to talk of old times in Russia and Italy. "I *won't* go now," said Moura, on her way to the telegraph office, as if in rebellion against a compelling demand. I remembered that afterwards but at the time I was merely desirous that we should not be bothered by this irrelevant interruption. I had her word for it that there was a Great Friendship with Gorky and that was all that was between them. Nothing could come between us in this phase of our liaison.

We returned from Austria as far as Paris together and there I left her to look up her sister. She rejoined me in London a little while later and I began to go about with her as publicly as possible and to introduce her everywhere as the woman I wanted to marry. And now it was I began to lose sight of any reality about Moura; to give way to my imagination; to make a dream and a hope of her beyond all possibility and in fact to fall and display myself "head over heels" in love with her. A new and wonderful Moura I evolved against all the facts of the case; I exalted my love beyond recognition; and, when at last the huge bubble of expectation I had blown burst, I found the former Moura of our free uninquisitive intimacy had vanished in the process. We both wounded each other and left unforgettable sores and she unwittingly hurt me, far more than she was hurt.

We are still intimate (spring 1935) and we can flirt and make love together. Great friends we are and companionable at bed and board. But the April brightness has gone out of things and that temporary blaze of glory has vanished altogether.

What I wanted of her in that phase was, in the fullest sense, marriage. I wanted her to come completely into my life, to span my *persona* with her own, as our bodies spanned each other, to launch upon a great adventure together. I had a persuasion that the world had already come to a phase when my political conceptions could be crystallized into effective forms. I did not think that I myself could make a figure, as the phrase goes, in politics, but I believed I could contribute greatly to get a powerful drive of ideas going. I thought the time had come to use the film as a medium and that it could be so used long before the forces of repression could be used against it.

I wanted to go to America and talk my ideas into people, to go to Russia and talk the same ideas, to talk about Europe, and I thought that, with her and her perfect ease in nearly every important Western language and her lively and intelligent interest in politics, we might have made a great sowing. I thought her serenity of manner and her boldness would be of inestimable value in that joint adventure. With her companionship to exhilarate and sustain me, I felt I should have ten times the strength and assurance of my unsupported self. I set no limits to her possible help and inspiration in that dream of her. At last, I thought, I am mated.

But from the Austrian honeymoon onward, I found her extraordinarily indisposed to fall into this conception of wifehood and alliance. She was content with the fun and pleasure of our association, and she was fundamentally indifferent to my dream. She seemed blind to it and deaf to it. But maybe she was not so much blind as afraid of our power to sustain it.

We had some months of baffling relationship. I took her about to my friends; we went touring in the South and West of England together, we stayed together at Bournemouth for three weeks, and I showed her everywhere as the woman I wanted to marry. But with a quiet obstinacy she opposed and frustrated me. We stayed nearly a month in Bournemouth in January and February in 1934, and I should have stayed longer—I was planning then a propagandist film, *Things to Come*; and I did a broadcast on the world outlook there—but she was so obviously distracted, so anxious to have long telephone conversations with London, that I returned thither with her, already deeply disappointed and angry with her. I began to realize that though I was a delightful adventure for her and her official lover, she had a complex series of interests and affections which were in the aggregate far more real and vital to her than this high hard dream of mine. Her mind was living mainly in a world of Russian refugees, in her family affairs, in the *coulisses* of international journalism, in a network of associations with the activities of the past. She had intimates with whom she had shared prison and poverty. She moved, conscious of a certain predominance, in a world of queer characters, exiles and adventurers, borrowers and people in need of help. She likes to help; she likes to give. She was their "wonderful Moura" and she loved that easy rôle. She was still friendly also with a multitude of minor diplomatists and newspaper correspondents on the fringe of diplomacy, and people of the Bruce Lockhart quality; and she still saw politics from the angle of the embassy, the meeting, the paragraph and the anecdote. And she liked the business by which she made her living of selling translation rights and doing suchlike little deals. She had a pride in her independence. These things were realities to her, and, in comparison, the things I had in my mind did not seem to her to be real.

And she had habits that were growing upon her and taking hold of her much more effectively than I was doing. Whenever she found life a little dull or perplexing, whenever she felt the onset of doubt or indolence, she drank brandy. If life remained dull and perplexing, she drank some more. I did not realize how much her failure to adapt herself to my needs and respond to my appeals was assisted by this ready consolation.

I began to be exasperated and jealous. She went off to Estonia for Christmas; she explained that that was imperative, and I could not see the pre-eminence of that claim. "But I have always spent my Christmas in Estonia!" she said, and returned after three weeks.

"I want you to come to America with me," I said, "and to do that in comfort we must be married. We can't have our effect complicated by trouble on that score. And I want to go to Russia with you because in Russia without you I am blind. But with your eyes. . . . You made me see Russia in 1920. Why not now?"

She still resisted marriage, and she explained that it was impossible for her to go to Russia with me. She made me believe that Russia was a barred country to her. She looked me in the eye and told me that.

"I want to go to America and talk to Roosevelt," I said. "If you won't come with me, I must go alone."

She let me go alone in April and she went off east again to see, she said, after her Estonian affairs.

I returned from America, more set than ever on going to Russia and talking with Stalin. She reiterated the impossibility of her going to Russia with me, and I went with my son Gip in July 1934. I arranged to fly to Moscow, and, a week or so before I was to depart, we agreed that she should go to Estonia. Then I would come back from Russia and stay with her at her home near Tallinn and tell her all about the changes that had occurred there. I saw her off from Croydon. We parted very tenderly. I remember her face peeping smiling from the aeroplane window as the machine taxied off.

That was the last I ever saw of my dream of Moura as a probable collaborator in a great political adventure.

In Moscow I was hampered by my complete ignorance of Russian, and considerably bored and disgusted by the Intourist organization in which I was enclosed. I got rather ill and very irritable. I had the clumsy conversation with Stalin which I have described in my *Autobiography* and which was published in pamphlet form.

A day or so later I started out in a car to see and dine with Maxim Gorky in his great country-house. In the *Autobiography*

I have described the dreary argument we held about free expression. With me was Andreychin, who was my official guide, and Umansky, who had been my interpreter in my talk to Stalin. "How do you return to London?" said Umansky, in perfect good faith.

I said I was returning by way of Estonia where I was going to stay for some weeks with my friend the Baroness Budberg.

"She was staying here a week ago," said Umansky, not realizing the bomb he was exploding.

I was too stunned to conceal my astonishment. "But I had a letter from her in Estonia," I said, "three days ago!"

Andreychin intervened with an obvious warning to Umansky and the latter shut up like an oyster. "Perhaps I was mistaken," lied Umansky to my further enquiries.

I did what I could to collect my thoughts but the situation was a staggering one. I carried on my talk with Gorky, with a sort of expectation that suddenly Moura might come suddenly smiling round a corner to greet me. But she had skedaddled back to Estonia. Greeting me in Russia wasn't at all in her picture. I should have been in the way. I should have realized something or I should have spoilt something. As we went down to supper, I got Andreychin to say to Gorky, "I miss our previous interpreter, Gorky."

He was taken unawares. "Whom do you mean?"

"Moura," said I.

There was a hasty passage in Russian between Andreychin and Gorky. "Gorky says she has been here three times in the past year," said Andreychin. That, I checked up hastily, was Christmas and when I was in America. I had been told more than I expected to hear.

"Indeed," said I. "I didn't know that. I didn't know that at all."

The matter demanded some further talk in undertones. Presently Andreychin had to explain to me that there had to be a certain secrecy about Moura's visits to Russia, because it might embarrass her in Estonia and with her Russian friends in London. It would be better if I did not mention them to anyone. It was a hasty attempt to restore the shattered situation, but to me it did not seem to account for Moura's concealment of her visits from me. "Obviously," I said, as though that were the most ordinary request in the world.

So in an evening my splendid Moura was smashed to atoms. Why had she sneaked back to Moscow in this fashion? Why had she sneaked away again? Why had she told me nothing of this escapade? Why, if this adventure were an honest one, had she not awaited my coming and returned with me? Why, at any rate, had she not waited to greet me and find what she could do for me? Why had she let me tackle my difficulties alone? What false front would have been shattered if she and I had met in Gorky's household? What jarring incompatibilities would have appeared? I was rather a moody companion for Umansky and Andreychin during the long automobile ride through the summer night back to Moscow.

I never slept for the rest of my time in Russia. I was wounded excessively in my pride and hope. I was wounded as I had never been wounded by any human being before. It was unbelievable. I lay in bed and wept like a disappointed child. Or I prowled about in my sitting-room and planned what I should do with the rest of my life, that I had hoped so surely to spend with her. I realized to the utmost that I had become a companionless man.

"Why did you do this to me, Moura?" I said ever and again. "Why did you do this to me, you fool?"

I sat at my desk, a great clumsy carved desk, looted from some pre-revolutionary palace and with solid huge supports and fittings of brass and stone, planning what I should do. I had some excess of vindictiveness. I wrote to cancel the reservations I had made for a leisurely return together from

Estonia through Sweden and the Gotha Canal. I made that journey alone. I made a codicil to my will, cancelling the very considerable provision I had made for her, and got it witnessed at the British Embassy when I lunched there next day. I wrote to cancel the guarantee of a banking overdraft I had given to make things easy for her in London. I had various engagements in Sweden and Norway, and it seemed best that I should fly back from Leningrad to Stockholm, spending there the three weeks I had marked for Estonia. All my correspondence had gone to Estonia and some of it was urgent. I wrote and destroyed one or two letters to her. In such exercises I spent my Moscow nights; the dawn would break in upon me sitting there. The strain was complicated by the fact that through some humbugging agents' intrigue that had nothing to do with this Moscow situation I was under pressure to complete delivery of copy for the concluding chapter of my *Autobiography* from Estonia within three weeks; that stuff too had to be written; and so I was a jaded spectator of all the half-baked wonders Soviet Russia had to show me by day. In the end I decided to see Moura again face to face in Estonia. I sent her a postcard saying I had heard a preposterous rumour that she was in Moscow and giving the date of my arrival at Tallinn. So I gave her a faint intimation of the questions she would have to answer.

She met me at the airport at Tallinn, candid-seeming, self-possessed and affectionate. She kissed me. "You look tired, my dear. Your eyes are tired."

"Dog-tired I am of most things, Moura. And I do not like your new Russia."

"You must come home and rest with me."

We dropped my bags in the Balts' Club in the town and drove to a restaurant on the outskirts to get some lunch, for the train to take us to Kallijarov where she lived did not go until the afternoon.

I had visited Tallinn when it was still called Reval in 1920, before our first meeting, and I compared the impression I got of the town coming to it by day from an airport, with the memories of my landing from the steamer at the quay late at night.

Came a pause. "That was a funny story of your being in Moscow," said I.

"How did you hear it?"

"Just a fragment of talk. Was it at Litvinov's? Perhaps it was."

"I can't imagine."

"No."

But I couldn't go on with that sort of thing.

"Moura," I said, "you are a cheat and a liar. Why did you do this to me?"

She held herself together magnificently.

"I was going to tell you. It was arranged suddenly after I got to Estonia. Tania knows. Micky knows. They will tell you."

Tania was her daughter and Micky was her old Irish governess and companion.

"In Estonia where you had gone, as you said, to rest. Where you said you were lying fallow."

"It was arranged suddenly."

"And you left a letter to be posted to me in Moscow from Estonia."

"Let us go to lunch. We must lunch anyhow. Then I can explain."

"Yes," I said, and laughed. "You remember that picture in the *Illustration Français*; the wife disrobed; the disconcerted young guardsman putting on his trousers; the unexpected husband. 'Give me time,' she pleads, 'and I will explain *everything*.'"

"You're ill and tired," said Moura.

We sat over a great dish of crayfish and a bottle of white wine at a table in the shade of big trees. The habit of cheerful association was strong in us. "I like this little wine," I said, and then remembered our drama. "And now, Moura, for your explanation."

She explained that the occasion to go to Moscow had arisen suddenly. She had seen no harm in going. Gorky had arranged it with the Russian Foreign Office. She had wanted to see the country again.

"But why not have waited for me there? Why not have acted as my guide and helped me?"

"Because I couldn't be seen about in Moscow."

"You just went to Gorky."

"I went to Gorky. You know he is an old friend. I wanted to see Russia again. You don't know what Russia is to me. It would have put him wrong with the Party if I had been seen about at all. If I had been seen about with you it would have put everything all wrong. It would have put you wrong. It's fantastic—I always said it was fantastic—for you and me to think of going to Russia."

"But in Gorky's house you could have met me. No one would have known of that."

"I wanted to get back to prepare things for you here. I did not want to stay longer."

"And this was the first time you have visited Russia since you came out ten years ago to Estonia. That must have been interesting. What did you think of it?"

"I was disappointed."

"Yes?"

"In Russia, in Gorky, in all sorts of things."

"Moura, why do you keep on lying? You have been three times to Russia in the past twelvemonth."

"No."

"You have."

"How can you think that?"

"Gorky told me."

"How could he? He doesn't know English."

"He told me through my interpreter, Andreychin."

"This is the first time I have been back to Russia since I came out to the children. Andreychin made some mistake in translation."

We stared at each other. "I wish I could believe you," I said.

And that was as far as we ever got in the business. I have remained wishing I could believe her and that I could wipe away the vestiges of that Moscow business which is like an open and incurable sore between us, ever since. The sore is on my mind; it is a recurrent fountain of distrust.

She stuck to it stoutly that she had been to Moscow only once. I had misunderstood or Andreychin had misunderstood. As I knew, she reminded me, she had seen the Gorky family in Warsaw after she had left Sorrento and once before that in Berlin. But these were not meetings in the past twelvemonth. Gorky may have said she had visited him and Andreychin may have thought it meant visited him in Russia.

"In the last year," I said, chewing it over.

"Anyhow you didn't care what sort of trouble I had in Russia," I reflected. "And it didn't matter a damn to you that I was there for the first time after our first wonderful meeting in 1920. But listen, because this is supremely important to me. I shall never believe you were not in Russia three times unless you clear up this story of the bad interpretation. I'm sorry, but that is how my mind will work. You can do it. You can write to Andreychin. You can get the whole thing explicitly stated. Get it clear. There is a telephone to Leningrad. You telephoned to me yesterday about the hour of my arrival. Get me through to him. And also I shall never be at peace in my mind until I know more clearly what your exact relations with Gorky are, how you stood to that son of his who died, and just what the relative importance of this side of your life is to you. I don't care a rap for anything that has been, so long as you come straight with me now. I've put my cards on the table with you, Moura, long ago; put *your* cards down. Come *to* me. Or am I nothing more to you than an adventure—one of a jumble of adventures?"

"You are the man I love," she said.

"That I had supposed—and it has been something tremendous to me."

She said she would get the matter of the misunderstanding cleared up. She had never been anything to Gorky but a friend; a great friend because he had done wonderful things for her when her life was in danger. Everybody knew—she threw in the information—that Gorky had been impotent for years. She had had only four days in Russia. (But I believed she had had ten.) I went to her home with her and that night she came to my room.

But that cleared up nothing. No lucidities came through from Andreychin and yet there was a good telephone service to both Leningrad and Moscow. And no clear explanation came of the whole business of her Gorky relationship, because it was plainly something that she had never explained even to herself. She has a vast series of whim systems in her motives; she has a number of incongruous relationships in her mind, and she has neither the mental simplicity nor the courage to tell me things as they were. Nothing in all this assuaged my distrust of her. We made love—but we had the canker of this trouble between us. I tried to pull things right by talking, but instead we walked through the woods quarrelling. This woman cannot explain herself, and I was too distressed to realize her inability. I was like a schoolmaster who punishes pupils for not suddenly understanding trigonometry. I scolded her and thought that then everything would come clear. I went off alone to Sweden in a bitter mood, just before her son celebrated his twenty-first birthday. I didn't want to be a wet blanket at the jollifications, and my temper was becoming untrustworthy. I was jealous of the son, of her visitors, of the Estonian house, of Russia. Above all of Russia. For some years my judgments on Russia have been *hard* and unjust on account of this. . . .

She came to see me off at Tallinn—like a lover, like the only lover in the world. For she loves partings and meetings; she does them superbly. We lunched at Tallinn and went to the Stockholm hydroplane together. At the last moment she declared her intention of joining me in Oslo.

She did that, but, as if in sympathy with the new phase in our relations, it rained steadily in Norway; it was Sunday in Bergen, and Sunday in Bergen would make a Scottish Sabbath seem frivolous, and we had a rough crossing of the North Sea—so that she kept her cabin, sea-sick, for she is a wretched sailor—and I meditated on deck alone.

And after that—

We have gone on together because of a real inability to part. She held on tenaciously (June 1935). But we were no longer the happy and confident lovers we had been, and I at least was profoundly discontented. From that time on I became exacting, and she was more and more femininely defensive.

I became exacting because now I was suspicious and jealous. I have always denounced this ugly condition of the mind in theory, but that did not prevent my suffering continuously after my Moscow shock for more than a year from this shameful mental disease. The attitude I tried to assume was a return to our former freedoms. Moura could still be a delightful associate and lover. What right had I to object even if she played little tricks on me and kept a good deal of her life and purposes hidden from me? She had never bound herself to do differently. Why not treat her too in the same way and keep our liaison light and happy?

I could not do that—just then. For a time I became more and more the uneasy husband. I became observant. I found myself checking her comings and goings, watching her—no longer for the delight of watching her but with a detective if not very penetrating eye. She did cheat. She did lie. Why, I asked myself, was she swathed in disingenuousness? Was it just pretty Fanny's way; her peculiar method of treatment, the feminine method of treatment? For my own good?

After our return to England in September 1934, I went to Bodnant and stayed with Christabel. We walked about those endless gardens and talked. I told her something of the things that were troubling me, and she unfolded a very prevalent feminine theory. "We all cheat," said Christabel. "We cheat you just as we have to cheat our children. Not because we don't love you, but because you are such unreasonable things that you would not let us live anything you could call a life if we didn't."

"That cuts both ways."

"Have I ever suspected you," she asked, "of telling me any more of the truth than suited your purpose at the time?"

"We all lie. Our very ideas of ourselves are protective and compensatory. And, my dear, is it always for *our* good—that feminine cheating?"

Well, we both knew it wasn't. We both had a very clear sense of the incurable complexity of individual life; its sustaining pretences and false simplifications. The invincible ego lies below mask after mask, even hiding from itself. Why go down to that? Why doubt that a woman has a heart until you have torn it out? No one, she said, could stand the ruthlessness of examination I was now applying to Moura. "Stick to her, H.G. and shut your eyes. I loved to see you together here when you came over from Portmeirion last summer. Of course you love each other. Isn't that good enough?"

But I cared too deeply for Moura to keep things at that

superficial level. I wanted her, skin and bones, nerves and dreams—or it seemed to me I did not want her at all. I could not be happy about the things below her masks. I wanted truth and true love there. I could not give her the benefit of the doubt.

Somewhen during this unhappy time at the end of 1934 I had a disagreeable dream. On this occasion as on other occasions in my life, the dream threw up, in a cruel and monstrously exaggerated form, just the ideas I had been holding down in my efforts to keep fair-minded and superficial and trustful. But before I tell the dream I must explain that very often after a theatre or a party Moura would come home with me and go to bed with me, and then, instead of dressing completely, she would slip on her dress and roll up her stays in a parcel and depart, smiling radiantly, thinly clad, with that scandalous parcel under her arm, and so by taxi home.

I dreamt I was wandering late at night in a certain vague strange evil slum—grotesque and yet familiar, which has been a sort of dream background in my mind for years—and I began to think of her, as I have thought of her so often in so many places, with longing, with a sort of heart-ache hope for her. Then suddenly, she was before me, my Moura, carrying that voluminous bag of hers.

"What's in that bag of yours?" said I and had seized upon it before she could resist.

And then, after the incoherent fashion of dreams, the bag having vanished, there appeared her stays wrapped in newspaper. In this slum!

"Who have you been with?" I cried, and forthwith I was beating her furiously. I was weeping and beating at her. She fell to pieces, not like a human being but like a lay figure, with hollow pasteboard limbs, and her head was a plaster thing that rolled away from me. I pounced upon it and it was hollow and had no brains in it. . . .

I woke up in a state of pale and dreadful anger and hate.

Once again, as I had done so often, I stared dismally at the night, going over the details and particulars of that Moscow deception. Even if the objections she made to going to Russia with me as my interpreter were valid, they still did not excuse her for her indifference to how I fared in Russia. If her relations to Gorky had the platonic quality she ascribed to them, she would have discussed my coming with him; she could have arranged for me to visit Gorky while she was there; even if it was undesirable that she should be known to have visited Russia; even if she could not appear publicly as my interpreter, she could have been with me in private; she could have been beside me to discuss my impressions; she could have made love in Russia once more; she could have returned to Tallinn with me. If she had been my true lover, that is what she would have thought of doing and wanted to do. That is what she would have done in 1920. Plainly her relations to Gorky—even if they were, as she declares, sexless—were of a nature so intimate and sentimental that she could not be with us together, in the same place. Probably, like so many copious-minded animated people, she was caught between two streams of relationship, two romanticized relationships, that she had failed to correlate. She would have had to repudiate something in herself, either on the one side or the other, and that was against her pride and disposition. Someone had to be sacrificed. And it was I in this case who was the person who had to be sacrificed and humbugged. Gorky had the satisfaction—if he wanted that satisfaction—of knowing she could make a fool of me for the sake of visiting him. She could let me suffer all the sterilizing exasperations of Intourist travel from which she might have saved me—in order to avoid a disturbance with him. Everything else was subordinated to that persuasion. I saw clearly I could never mitigate nor dissolve it away, and that Moura had no art to destroy it.

"That is where we stand," said I, "and nothing in earth or heaven can alter that now." A swarm of memories of close association and tender, delightful and passionate memories could do nothing against these iron facts.

I think that dream and the grey mood of my subsequent wakefulness was the culmination and end of my stormy struggle with what was at first an almost intolerable disappointment and disillusionment. It was decisive. It was a fantastic exaggeration to dream that dear and pretty head was plaster and empty—it was all too full and busy—but it was clear that my Moura was at best incoherent-minded, and as disingenuous as all instinctive incoherent-minded people must be. She liked and loved me, I had no doubt, I could have no doubt; but she did not love me simply, wholly and honestly. There was nothing in the world she loved simply, wholly and honestly. She said she was altogether faithful to me and probably she was. Certainly she thought she was faithful to me. The reveries in which I had indulged of a last good phase of living at the end of my life with a splendid mate beside me were lost in a swarming exaggerated realization of her defects; her small human greeds, her flashes of scheming, her innate slovenliness, her moments of vanity and her discontinuities. How can one trust a discontinuous mind that seems unaware of its inconsistencies? I asked. I forgot a thousand counter-vailing things; her courage, impulsive generosities, moments of great tenderness and flashes of wisdom.

A day or so after, I found her deceiving me about a small matter of no importance. I reproached her, and after her manner she denied the deception stoutly and earnestly. I had always been used to taking her asseverations in absolute good faith, but now I found I disbelieved her. Then I told her of my dream and of how I had lain and thought of her and what I had thought, and we took up again the long quarrel and struggle of will that had been flaming or smouldering between us since my first reproaches at Tallinn. She stood up in my study still defending herself and still not yielding me that complete frankness that alone could have restored our broken confidence and closeness in their old perfection.

"Why do you spoil everything by putting me on trial like this?" she said.

"Why did you make it so that I have to put you on trial?"

"But things aren't so," she said, with such resolution that it seemed she might even yet override the very facts.

It seemed to me that she was like some lovely animal caught in a net. It was none the less a net about her because it was of her own spinning. I could not break it for her and it was plain she would not break it for herself. I was as bitterly sorry for her as I was for myself. She had lost as well as I. The things for which she had belittled our love were worthless beside the unqualified love that had seemed within our grasp and that had slipped out of our grasp and broken.

"There's no more to be said about all this, my dear," I said, with some lurking feeling that still she might say or do some wonderful thing to save us.

I would not have cared what she had done or what had happened to her in the past; I would have helped her out of any complex or entanglement, if she had come through to me clear and plain. But she took it there was no more to be said, because she could not relinquish what she was reserving from me.

We kissed and made an end of discussing our unsolved tangle. We kissed and went to bed together. We said hardly anything more about it for some days. But there it lies between us. Everything about Moscow rests unexplained. Did she go thrice or once? I do not know. I begin to feel it does not matter. But the Moura who was never really there has vanished now for ever and nothing in earth or heaven can bring her back. We were still lovers as the word goes, and intimate associates.

We could still laugh and talk about a thousand things. But we were consciously apart from each other. We were sitting back to look at each other.

I recurred to the sore point time after time. I could not keep off it. She wept—with anger. She acted a great parting, said "Goodbye," went out and banged my study door and so out of the flat. In five minutes she was back, hammering at the outer door.

"Escape me never," said I, admitting her ruefully. "Escape you never. I knew you would come back."

She took refuge at last in a formula.

"You are sadistic," she said, pacing my room. "You are cruel."

"I'm driving you to see yourself?". . . .

I would puzzle over that accusation of cruelty. Was I perhaps tormenting her while she herself was struggling towards me? Maybe in the past she had had an imaginative obsession for Gorky and Russia that was weakening. She might be trying consciously and sub-consciously to get to me and she did not know how to do it and she was divided in her mind. She had the feminine and childish weakness of expecting complete and instinctive apprehension of things she could not in any way make clear. She did not know how to give in to anyone, and the luck of the situation had put her in the wrong and turned her lover into an accuser. Were there things she expected me to understand without admission from her? Did she expect a tacit pardon without expressed repentance? Did she think I comprehended—and ought to forgive and forget and begin again?

But then there were those other petty deceptions, little bits of humbug, little "lets down" just sufficient to spoil the picture for my now over-sensitized scrutiny.

We had three months of such unrest and intermittence to the end of 1934. In December we decided to go off together to

Palermo with the idea of getting closer, alone in a novel setting; but a breakdown in the Italian air service stranded us at Marseilles and we stayed upon the Riviera rather than face the tedious railway journey to Sicily. Christmas week we spent in Somerset Maugham's Villa Mauresque.

I found that I was uneasy and jealous and critical of her. My former pride in her was tainted and our former confidence gone. We had some good times and some hard-eyed moments. I had a habit of waking at seven or before and she would lie in bed until ten or eleven. Conversely she wanted to be amused into the small hours. With conversation and drink—that backbone-less, fluid, well-informed, un-analytical Russian conversation that wanders everywhere and gets nowhere, and drink to make it glow. To fill in the slack of three or four morning hours I set to work making a film treatment of my short story, *The Man Who Could Work Miracles*, and I found it went very well. I found my imagination in a renascent state and that quite a number of fresh ideas were cropping up in my mind. I was developing a new life in that solitary morning freshness.

Then abruptly she wanted to go back to England because of her children; she wanted to see to her son's outfit for college and her daughter, she said, wanted her in some stress of feeling. That caused another quarrel in which the demands of my egotism showed themselves hard and intolerant. "Here am I," I scolded, "launched on a good piece of work and happy with you, and you want to flit off again and leave me stranded and alone in this damned hotel. Your Paul is of age, and when you were Tania's age you had divorced a husband. Let them work out their own problems. This is how you always leave me. You leave me about. You don't care what becomes of me. . . ."

And so on. A real husband's rowing.

She went implacably, leaving me in a fever of resentment,

and a day after, I had a note from an American widow who owned race-horses and whom I had met at lunch at Maugham's. I cannot imagine a less descriptive phrase than "American widow." She was rather like Moura physically; west to her east, tall and dark and smiling, explicit where Moura was implicit, slender and fit where Moura was slack. I cannot convey the refreshment of her explicitness. She was very freckled and the golden patches suited her. Most of her early education she had had in tow of her wealthy and fitful mother; the father had been taken round the world for a time and then "parked." It was an extremely informal education. She retained a pleasant American frankness and simplicity; she had heard from Maugham that I was alone at the Hermitage Hotel, and she asked me in a schoolgirl handwriting to come to dinner with her at the Negresco.

I had already liked a simple directness about her at our first encounter, and that evening I found her naïve and experienced and entertaining. She was living an oddly orderly and industrious life at Nice—the funniest life by my standards. It was, so to speak, a residium of the things that had chanced to her. She was as fond of the morning sunshine as Moura disliked it, and she would be out walking her "dorg" before breakfast. After her coffee she would sit down with her newspapers and a heap of special notes and reports, and work, industriously and competently, for three hours, upon the "form" of the current horse-racing. Her knowledge, I am assured, was wide and competent, shrewd and profound. Equipped for the fray she went out—if there was a race-meeting—to bet, or if there was not a race-meeting, then, with a system she had come to believe in, an extremely tedious and boring system (which carried her along for a number of weeks and then let her down), to the Casino. She lunched and dieted with great discretion, so that her mind should not be heavy and confused for these grave duties. Her social occasions were incidental to these activities. Towards dinner-time she might relax with a cocktail.

She was not a talker in public, but she sat listening very brightly and understanding very quickly. In private she talked most entertainingly, very frankly and with keenly appreciated detail. She did not go out very much, and generally she dined alone in the hotel, and gave herself up to reading. She read widely, with a wide-eyed curiosity, and her commentary was naïve and shrewd and "illiterate" as only America's commentary can be. She had none of that façade of culture an educated European woman is given as a matter of course. Passages she liked, she copied out in an unformed schoolgirl hand. She was struggling with Dunne's book on *Immortality* and some book, I forget which, by Whitehead. She was not above taking Spengler seriously. She had Bertrand Russell's book by her and she was reading, with the acutest understanding, *The Letters of Katherine Mansfield.* Fiction she liked and criticized penetratingly, except that she found detective stories too metallic and artificial. We set together very interestingly and anatomized a volume of T.S. Eliot's poems. She knew and felt infinitely more than I did about modern poetry, but I don't think she had the faintest inkling that that was how things were between us.

When we had dined together at that first meeting and talked of books and immortality and love and what was to be put into life and what was to be got out of it, and come to a point when I should have left the Negresco for my rooms at the Hermitage, I stood up to go and it seemed to be the most natural thing in the world to take her in my arms and kiss her and for her to kiss me back—and after that I did not go for an hour or so.

Thereafter for a week we were together for as much as we could be. We just liked being together. I would do my "work" and she would do her "work" until midday, and then her Hispano Suiza would be at my door and, with a sense of virtuously spent time behind us, we would be off to some amusing restaurant. We would go up into the mountains or along the coast. In the evening we explored the variety of dinners to be found in Nice, and I took her to eat *bouillabaisse* in the old town. Also there were cinemas which she took very seriously.

But now suddenly Moura decided to return to me. Perhaps she thought of me in a pathetic state of devotion at the Hermitage, or perhaps some instinct of possession told her not to leave me about too long. Or, most probable thing of all, she did not think about what I was doing at all and only just wanted to be with me again. I made no suggestion that she should return. She wired: "If I do not hear from you I shall return on Wednesday." But some complication of dates or engagements intervened and, to Moura's considerable astonishment, I answered: "Saturday will be more convenient." She telegraphed "Always at your convenience," and came on Saturday.

"What have you been up to?" asked Moura when she arrived.

"Friendship," said I.

She was not so much jealous as amused and on her mettle. The three of us met, and we got on extremely well together. We made excursions; we lunched and dined together and went over to Maugham's to lunch. To the vivid interest of Maugham. Moura watched me closely and unobtrusively. "I have never seen you visibly in love with anyone else before," she said.

"It's good for you," I said.

"You look at each other. You watch her. You make her feel worth while."

"You ought to know," I said.

We arranged to return by road as far as Paris. But it chanced that Moura did not come with us. A telegram came from Estonia that Micky—Mrs. Wilson, her old governess and the governess of her children—was very ill and was asking for her. This was no trick. I found Moura and the telegram. She was blubbering with her knuckles in her eyes, like a miserable little girl. "Poor Micky," she said, "poor dear Micky."

"You can go to her."

"You'll be *e*ngry again if I go."

"You'll never forgive yourself if Micky dies," I said, and I helped her to pack and start off upon the long train journey to Estonia. And a day after I went off to Paris by road in the Hispano Suiza.

We spent the night at the celebrated hotel, the Hôtel de France, I think it is, at Mâcon, where the Kaiser's former cook still ruled the kitchen. There I found a telegram from Moura awaiting me with one word "Love."

"Is that an injunction?" I said.

"We don't need an injunction. Isn't this a *nice* dinner?"

In the morning coffee and rolls seemed inadequate and we had a couple of boiled eggs each and I sat on her bed and cut off their heads and showed her how to eat them in the English fashion, and so we went on very gaily to Paris. And next morning I flew to London.

Moura was away in Estonia and I was quite sure she had gone there for the single purpose of nursing Micky, but I knew that if there was any delay in her return to England there was a strong risk that all the old resentments and suspicions would return. I was doing my best to put them in the background of my imagination, and when presently a proposal came from *Colliers Weekly* in New York for me to spend three weeks in America and write about the New Deal. I accepted. I arrived early in March 1935; I lunched with the President in Washington and talked to all sorts of people; I had a very good time, and I wrote four articles which were published later as a book, *The New America: The New World.*

Now this trip to America would, I thought, help that emotional detachment from Moura to which my affair was contributing. But I found her still troubling my mind very greatly. I began thinking of her again as my lovely dream Moura; I wanted to have her with me on the boat; to show her New York and talk of all the amusing differences of America, and whenever I went to a party or reception I wanted her beside me.

I felt more and more exasperated to be alone. My anger mounted at the failure of Moura to realize my desire for her companionship. It infuriated me that for my sake she would not rouse herself from that petty squalid exile life of hers; the endless gossip, the higgledy-piggledy of 88 Knightsbridge, the too much vodka, the too much brandy, the lying in bed until midday and the chatting nocturnalism. I was angry with her too because she had made it possible for me to be unfaithful to her and that I was likely to slip back to promiscuity. In Washington I was reminded at one or two parties that women could be attractive to me and seem attracted by me.

These experiences made me more and more determined to grapple with Moura or break with her. Here again, I thought, is what I want. Here is the way out for me. I wrote Moura an ultimatum. "Either come into my life completely," I wrote, "or get out of it. Cut out all there is in your life that comes between us. Either meet me at Southampton in token of entire submission or send back the latchkey you have to my flat."

There was no Moura at Southampton, but I was hardly back in London when she rang me up. Her throat was very much worse, she explained, and she was ill in bed. Would I come to her? That was an unexpected setting for the return of the latchkey.

I sat on her bed, resisting my habitual urge to caress her, and she talked of Micky's illness and her own. She had had a bout of pneumonia at Kallijarov herself but she hoped to get up betimes. She was blandly ignoring my ultimatum, just as in Estonia she had blandly ignored my demand for lucidities. She behaves at times exactly after the fashion of my black cat at Lou Pidou who never had a doubt in the world—whatever his misdeeds—that he had only to get up on the table beside me, rub his face against mine; and do and get exactly as he pleased.

Next day she rang me up. "We ought to talk," she said, "where shall we lunch?"

I did not want her to come to my flat and so I arranged to meet her at the Serbian Restaurant in Greek Street. She seemed wonderfully recovered.

"And now, dear," she said gravely, when we had lunched, "shall we go back to Chiltern Court?"

We went back to Chiltern Court.

Her face was a foot from mine on the pillow and she looked at me with a gleam of mischief in her sleepy eyes.

"You were in love with her," she said.

"I am in love with nobody," I said. "Or everybody. I gave you myself in a lump and you have scattered me again to the winds of heaven. And here we are—what is left of either of us. We shall never marry now and yet I have never felt so completely and damnably married to anyone in my life."

The detailed history of my relations to Moura draws towards its end. My ultimatum died away and the latchkey was not returned. She stuck to it stoutly. But presently I set about finding myself a house in Hanover Terrace, Regent's Park, and began to plan a home for my concluding years in that pleasant situation. But I made no arrangements whatever for Moura in it.

"Shall I devote a floor to you and Tania and Paul with your own sitting-room and your own bell?" I asked in a last lapse towards my marriage dream. "We can still arrange that."

"Darling," she evaded, "haven't we gone into all that?"

"Very well," said I. "Stick to 88 Knightsbridge and all that it means to you. Soon they will pull that place down to build flats and all you Russians will be scattered like earwigs from under a stone. You'll collect together somewhere else, I suppose, after your fashion. But I tell you there will be no latchkey for you to Hanover Terrace—and don't blame me if you don't like that."

But Moura will never believe the door is bolted upon her until she finds it bolted and hammers on it in vain. And it will be impossible for me to make her hammer in vain. I suppose when she hammers I shall let her in—but always just a little more estranged.

(And in fact—I add in July 1936—she got her latchkey to the new house when in May she returned the one that let her into Chiltern Court.)

Maybe there is a limit to estrangement just as there is an aphelion set to the path of a planet. I doubt if we shall ever have quite done with each other. There is an irrational gravitation between us.

We seem destined to remain in this state of loose association, like double stars that rotate about each other but never coalesce. Our very looseness now averts a conclusive rupture. We are held together by habits and usages which wax and wane. It is absurd to say I am still in love. And yet I love—after a fashion. I doubt if we love each other very much, continuously and steadily. We still have phases of intense companionship and satisfaction with each other. And pride and ownership. Still. She likes to hear me praised and I like to hear her praised.

That was written in June 1935. In August Moura went to Estonia and I wrote to her from England rehearsing all my reasons for a permanent break between us in a number of brutally frank letters. She replied affectionately. "Why do you write such unkind things?" she seemed to consider a full reply to my indictments. She returned in September to resume our relations with her invincible imperturbability. She appeared suddenly at a reception I was giving to the Institute of Journalists in my capacity of President of the P.E.N. Club, of which she is also a member. When I saw her coming up the room to me with that serene face of hers and a gleam of affectionate wickedness in her eyes, I was glad. We were both glad. . . .

Eighty-eight Knightsbridge was pulled down in due course, and in the autumn of 1935 the group of refugees, to confute my prophecy, fell on their feet very comfortably at 81 Cadogan Square.

Much of the foregoing may read like an indictment of Moura. But if so, I am unjust to have phrased it in that way. So far as it is an indictment, it is an indictment of life, of the misfit of male and female desires and methods. It is one individual aspect of the general trouble between modern man and woman, complicated by the profound difference between the thought idiom of an intricate Russian, capable of blackening out anything in her memory she does not like, and that of a mind accustomed to intellectual consistency. It is also a statement of my own unreasonable monstrous demands for a Lover-Shadow, based on the exacting enormity of the *persona* I have devised for myself. I am, I know, trying to be something too big for my powers. I am an insufficient and often irritable "great man" with an infantile craving for help.

My story of my relations with women is mainly a story of greed, foolishness and great expectation, and it would not be worth the telling if it were merely my particular story. But it is really a tale of a world of dislocated sexual relations and failure to adjust. From Moura in my last phase as from Isabel in my first, I asked impossible things. I wanted a world-interested woman to my world-interested man. I wanted a match for the colour of my own mind—what is it?—priggishness, fanaticism, modernity, religion? Jane had it. I wanted a mate at my job. But Moura never pretended to want more than a romantic sexual and personal intimacy with me; a coming and a going based on preference and pleasure, and, until I left Odette and turned upon her, demanding marriage, home and an inseparable alliance, our meetings were always brightly happy. In that phase we neither of us enquired too closely into the doings of the other when we were apart; and we tolerated the amplest imaginative and emotional reserves. And when I faced round upon her and tried to take complete possession of her, saying that she had to be fully and completely *my* Moura, and to fuse everything in her life with me—and I with her—she was quite clear-headed and explicit in her defence of her private self and of all her habits and indolences and indulgences from my harsh and eager invasion. She knew she could not satisfy my demand anyhow. So why should she attempt to satisfy my demand?

I have told that Moura deceived me, but at least she has never deceived me about having reservations from me. She has never pretended to have given me all and shown me all. But I feel that, since we were lovers, there was an implication, as it were, of naked truth, and of self-abandonment. That is the utmost I can charge her with.

Since that Moscow crisis we have walked about in Estonia, in France, in England, in woods and forests and fields and great gardens, disputing and wrestling with each other, no longer the carefree lovers we used to be, exploring each other's affections delightfully as we used to do, and inventing pleasant things to say to each other. We have lost that lovely artificiality; the frank, exciting, sincere falseness, the bluff of love-making. Our affection, our pity for each other, may have deepened, our helpfulness maybe, and our mutual toleration. But to get to know each other so much more intimately than we did before, through accusations, injuries and quarrels and disillusionments, has not been to achieve any unanimity of bearing in our outlook. It has been rather to lay bare our immense incompatibilities and console rather than compensate each other for them.

Latterly there has been less disputation. We have worked that out. We have said everything there is to say—many times. I have come to agree with her that we must never marry; that we see quite as much of each other as it is good for us to see, and that our relationship must be left open to divergence. I do not know how far we shall diverge before we die. I do not count on her and she would be rash to count on me. And yet—inexplicably we still belong to each other (summer 1935).

(Rebecca, by the by, has hit upon something of this same sort of belongingness in a very good short story of hers, "Life Sentence," in her book *The Harsh Voice*.)

These oscillations between attraction and separation destroy my hopes of a busy and united home, but they do not destroy my desire for a home. I still dream of living with a wife, my wife, in a house and garden of my own. I want that still; it is unreasonable but it is what I want; and I see I shall never get it. I am tired of this flat and Moura's latchkey into the heart of my days.

I don't want to go about with a woman who has to be explained and who will not go or cannot go round the wide world with me. I wanted my wife to be of the same religion as myself, to have in her mind, that is, a real fanaticism for the perhaps unattainable world-state I serve, and I do not want our desires and amusements to be at war with the rational purpose of my life. I wanted that woman to be patient with me and not restless when I was preoccupied. I wanted her to have work of her own and work that I could respect, so that I could be patient with her. We would have had the house and garden in common and we would have eaten together and played together and worked in harmony together, and when we wanted change or stimulation we would have gone off to travel together or to visit London and all our many friends, who are so much more real, more stereoscopic and satisfying and amusing, when they are seen not flatly with a single eye but through convergent lenses. I wanted to feel a dear presence always in my home with me, to hear a beloved voice upstairs or to look out of the window and see my own dear coming up the garden to me.

But Moura will never come up that garden because, through her incurable vagrancy, there will never be that garden, our garden about *our* house. It is the Lover-Shadow of my *persona* I want in the garden of my desires; and that is not Moura now, I realize, but Jane plus Moura plus fantasy—a being made up of a dead woman, a stimulating deception and the last dissolving vestiges of imaginative hope. There is no right nor reason in my wanting this, but this is the common dream of the normal active man who still has work to do.

Nature has not bothered to produce any special consolations for her creatures, after her own vague ends have been fulfilled by them. There is no last phase with its distinctive happiness in a man's life. If we want that we must make it for ourselves. I can still entertain imaginative hope. All my imagination did not die at Moura's feet. But I doubt if there is any other woman now for me in the world. Friendship perhaps may still be mine, a little fresh love-making perhaps, but not even the delusion of possession. I am sprung. I cared for Moura too much and I cannot begin again in real earnest to create another vital intimacy. At least that is how I feel now.

I have, I realize, still to master this last phase of life. It may after all be a new distinct phase, and in a fit of despondency I may be doing Nature an injustice in saying that she has no biological use for us after the love-cycle is over. I feel the work I am doing now is worth while (August 1935).

This "Postscript to *Experiment in Autobiography*" is becoming more and more of an intimate diary. I shall do little to change what has gone before, and much that I write here by way of conclusions may prove to be very provisional before the last pages are done.

§10
Shadow of Age: the Suicidal Mood

ON THE WHOLE and usually I am still not an unhappy person. If I am never now radiantly happy, I can for a time dispel the gathering shadows of loneliness and hopelessness by a spurt of activity. I have cut out enough work for myself to be able at any time, in the night or in the day, to turn my mind away from despair and a desperate conclusion. I get up, put some warm night-clothes on, and set about it. Nevertheless I am not safe from occasional attacks of acute misery. These may happen anywhen in the day-time or the night. Sometimes I am too fagged to work or sleep and then I have no refreshment at hand any more. I stare existence blankly in the face. I feel no incentive to action. I fear for the world then unreasonably and I am dissatisfied almost beyond endurance with everything.

These phases may be partly pathological in origin; an aspect of the diabetic diathesis; but none the less they have to be dealt with. When they are present they are present as states of mind and they have to be dealt with—at least so far as the moment goes—mentally. My Lover-Shadow has dispersed again and there is no one to whom I can go with the assurance of that envelopment and refuge and comfort for which the distressful heart craves. In my less protected moments I do think quite deliberately of self-destruction, either by open, deliberate suicide, which would be a frank confession that life has been too much for me; that it is not good enough and that I am beaten, and I and my universe a failure; or else furtively by letting go the innate weakness of my body and dying, as I could do, of my diabetes after a few months of self-indulgent illness—or still more easily perhaps by an encouraged pneumonia. This last would be the equivalent in my case of what is so frequent a method of retreat from the stress of life, "taking to drink."

I don't however do anything of the sort. I have never yet suffered so much that I have not had the spirit left to resist and attack my depression, and presently recover buoyancy. I carry on. If some day I should choose to swallow a score of aspirin tablets or anything of that sort, it will be the most exceptional and uncharacteristic aberration; it will express nothing, and I set this down here now; it will be an accident, some lump of despondency will have hit me like a meteorite from outer space. It will be an incident of senility, or a mind clot like that blood clot which caught in my father's heart-strings and finished him.

Normally I am incapable of suicide. I am of an absolutely opposite temperament to the melancholic. For most of the years of my life my mind has admitted quite unflinchingly the greater possibility of defeat for all I am and all I value; the immense threat of disaster in human affairs; and my philosophy has been the philosophy of a cheerful fight against the odds, possibly quite heavy odds. It has never seemed to me an adequate reason for desisting, that it is highly improbable that my world-state or any such human recovery will ever come true. All the more reason, it has seemed to me, for doing one's utmost. And since that is what I have preached and preached, arousing a response of stoical heroism in I know not how many other kindred minds, it is plain that any voluntary lapse from the pose and bearing of vital obstinacy on my part, simply because of a certain transitory weariness and recession of hope, would be the meanest of betrayals.

The most conclusive argument for suicide I find in my mind is the conviction of my own unworthiness. For that there is something to be said. Sometimes I realize something in myself so silly, fitful and entirely inadequate to opportunity, that I feel even by my own standards I am not fit to live. I am moved to throw myself away in sheer disgust. The experiment is over in substance, I feel then; the dregs of life do not matter. But then I reflect that though I have at last found myself out to this ultimate degree, there are a lot of other people who do not know my fundamental unsoundness and exhaustion and who do hold to me and by me. What are they going to make of such a suicide?

There may be a moral obligation to bear oneself as being better than one is. Disciples are creditors and must have their due. I think it would be extremely bad too for everyone in my family and personal group if I stepped out of life of my own accord. It isn't so much that they need any help or protection from me. It would not hurt any of them very much now if I died as a gentleman should, trying all the time to get better. Or if I were killed in an accident, fair and square. I have no excuse in my dependants for avoiding reasonable danger. But to go wilfully would leave a nasty sudden hole under their feet—I do not like to think of them staring down into such a chasm. . . .

And in short in that direction there is no way out for me. I have to stick life out through these fitful organic depressions. And I have no religious anaesthetics available. I just have to stick it out past the dreary points.

When first written, in early May 1935, this section ended as above. In

June my father added two paragraphs about his recovery from "that dip towards suicide into which my disillusionment with Moura carried me." These he removed from this position in July, to use them as the seeds from which the "Looseleaf Diary" was to grow.

The first of these seeds was the paragraph now on p. 205, beginning with "In May 1935 I began a sort of analysis and sublimation of these moods of disappointment and despair." The second was the one now on p. 206, beginning with "I have been playing with the idea of writing the film story as a literary form." [G. P. W.]

CHAPTER THE SECOND

THE LAST PHASE

§1
Looseleaf Diary

In May 1935 I began a sort of analysis and sublimation of these moods of disappointment and despair that come to imaginative men at the ebb, under the title of *The Anatomy of Frustration*. It is a modernized *Anatomy of Melancholy*. I am working upon it now (summer 1935), but as I write I do not know how far I may be able to make an effective thing of it. I want to survey the whole process of contemporary frustration and distil what courage and stimulus I can for myself and others from that survey. Perhaps this will give me a new form of expression through which I can not only get the better of my own bad moods but develop a new creative interest. There is, I feel, the possibility of an interesting book in that title and idea.

And in October 1935 I note that I have found this expectation realized and that the book has turned out well and served its purpose in clearing my mind. I shall hold it for revisions for a time, and publish it, I think, in 1936.

To which I add in January 1936 that this book still grows in bulk and in my estimation.

And in February that it seems to me nearly completed and that I am satisfied with it. I am giving parts of it an airing in the *Spectator*, to see what comment it arouses.

April 6th, 1936 finds this *Anatomy of Frustration* finished almost to the last comma and the last verbal correction. It has purged my mind enormously. It is a real step forward in my attempt to state my world. And yet—it isn't quite good enough. Shall I *never* get this thing that I am always saying properly said?

I realize more clearly every day that it is the work which *The Anatomy of Frustration* attempts to grasp completely and summarize which makes me a significant individual. The bulk of this "Postscript" deals only incidentally with that. The rest I might call "Personalia," and turns upon the chance encounters, the luck of life. These things colour life; make one hopeful, unhappy, well and ill, kill or enable; but they have little to do with the intrinsic difference of one's interpretation of life and one's fundamental good.

I have been playing with the idea of writing the film story as a literary form. The actual production of a film involves a thousand vexations and disappointments. I am not sure yet whether I shall be able to fight very effectively on the studio floor and in the cutting-room to realize my conceptions, though I do put up a fight, but I think I can so write the film for publication in book form that it will have an increasingly compelling influence on the actual production. That may prove a roundabout way to the mastery I want. The unworked possibilities of significance in the modern film, and its latent powers, are more enormous than I thought at the beginning, and such exploratory work is very much in my line. Here is another expanding interest from which I may still derive incentive and essential peace of mind in these concluding years. I am, I perceive, recovering week by week from that dip towards suicide into which my disillusionment with Moura carried me.

Already in August 1935 I find myself shaping into the life of these new interests, and Moura recedes more and more from her predominance in my imaginative life. She is away in Estonia and I hardly miss her at all nor care what she is doing. We have written each other four or five short un-love-letters. I have been living in the pretty house and garden of my son Frank at Digswell Water Mill while his family is away. The place has a water-garden made from the old mill stream, and there is a very pleasant summer pavilion with a divan to which I can carry a blanket in the moonlight these hot nights and sleep and dream. I have hired a car and renewed my interest in motoring; I run across country and spend more and more confident and effective days among the varied and interesting throng at the Cinema Studios at Isleworth and Denham. I have resumed one or two old intimacies and begun a fresh one.

I shall go to New York in October with films very much in mind and perhaps I shall fly over to Hollywood. I do not know when I shall come back to England. I may winter in California. . . .

At the end of October 1935 I add a note to say that I have booked my passage to America for November 7th, and that my suicidal phase seems to have passed completely. I was and am still interested in the film as a means of expression rather than entertainment. Both *Things to Come* and *The Man Who Could Work Miracles* developed a certain strength—more than I thought they could. They were fairly satisfactory to do, and Alexander Korda became a congenial colleague. (Disillusionment later, 1936.) I made him two other film stories, one a treatment of my old *Food of the Gods* and the other an expansion of a short story of mine, *The Story of the Late Mr. Elvesham*, which I think of calling *The New Faust*. These were to be made in 1936 and I was fairly content with both of them. They would, I thought, be hard to spoil in production. . . .

I crossed to America on November 7th, 1935, as I had intended.

I stayed for a few days with G. P. Brett of the Macmillan Company downtown, and then flew to Hollywood over the Grand Canyon and stayed there at the home of Charlie Chaplin for five weeks, visiting film studios and learning very much about film production and film finance. I had a rejuvenating time in the Californian sunshine. I visited the Hearst ranch, Cecil B. de Mille's ranch and Palm Springs. I ceased to think of myself as a disappointed and concluded man. I flew back on Christmas Day—the plane got iced and I had a day and a half on the train from Dallas onward by Washington to New York.

As I walked down the Waterloo platform on my return to London in January 1936, dodging the cameramen and the reporters, I suddenly saw Moura ahead of me, chin up and with that faint smile of hers, assured of herself and her particular world, tall and welcoming. Just as she had come to meet me at Salzburg and on the flying-ground at Tallinn—after Moscow. She had come to escort me to my flat.

"Escape you never," I said, kissing her.

"Have you t*rr*ied?" she asked.

"It was why I went to America," I said.

"You've been unfaithful to me again?"

"To the very best of my ability."

"You are fickle, you know," said Moura.

"The mountains of Arizona," I said, "are the loveliest I have ever seen."

"Did you go there with anyone?"

"A man who begins to answer questions is lost. Nevertheless the answer to that particular question, so far as the essence to your enquiry goes, is 'No,'"

"Then it was in Connecticut. . . ."

I asked after her children. But my manner made it suddenly plain to both of us that the incredible had happened and that the last traces of my long imaginative obsession with her had vanished. She had come down to life-size. It did not matter in the least that she came home with me and ate and slept with me that night. All exaltation was at an end. I felt for her now almost exactly as I had felt for that great black cat of mine, with its caresses and its fondling confidence, that I had left behind me so reluctantly at Lou Pidou. There was no animosity left now and no exaltation, but a great friendliness.

We were talking the other day: "You take no decent care of yourself," I said. "You do really drink too much. It is a pity you cannot be sent back to prison for a bit—as a treatment. You are becoming lazy and sluggish. I am a prophet. I know what the end of our affair will be. When I am old and shrunken and thin-voiced, you will fall ill upon me and die. Yes, you will, with no real consideration for me at all. You will eat and drink when you have been told not to do so, and that will end you. I shall come, poor old gentleman, and sit by your bedside every day. I have that much sense of obligation. I shall bring you flowers and things to make you think I still love you and keep you in a good conceit with yourself. I've always been too tender about that. I shan't know why I shall do it, but I know I shall."

"You love me."

"I shall never remind you then of how feckless you have been, how you have undermined me and consumed and wasted me."

"Hoo. Hoo."

"I shall make your dying a very pleasant retirement for you. I shall probably get double pneumonia at your funeral. You won't be cremated like a decent person. You insist upon being buried and you will as usual have your way. The day will be cold and wet. Yes, it *will* be. It will be like you to contrive things like that. I shall see you off for the last time and I shall go home rather deadened and nestling into my overcoat with the first intimations of my final chill."

"But before all that happens you must let me play the fat woman in Charlie Chaplin's version of *Mr. Polly*, as you said the other day."

"It is all you are fit for. But I believe you will let me down even over that. You will get ill or go to Estonia in the middle of the shooting."

Pause.

"Darling. Why do you always *reason* about love and misjudge me so?"

Her inconsecutiveness is invincible.

In this wry affectionate toleration ends the story of my amatory life. I was never a great amorist, though I have loved several people very deeply. I have tried to give as much as I can of how Moura stands to me and I stand to her. I have tried to reproduce our sort of conversation. I have recited all her faults and failings and misdeeds so far as I know them. In telling that I have revealed my own. And the fact remains quite clear—I think perhaps I have made it quite clear—that when all is said and done, she is the woman I really love. I love her voice, her presence, her strength and her weaknesses. I am glad whenever she comes to me. She is the thing I like best in life. In the last resort, in this sort of love, the rights and wrongs of the case are interesting but they do not alter the deep primary fact to any material degree. She is my nearest intimate. Even when I have let my vexation with her take the form of an infidelity, or when she has behaved badly to me and driven me to anger and reprisals, she has remained still the dearest thing in my affections. And so she will remain to the end. I can no more escape from her smile and her voice, her flashes of gallantry and the charm of her endearments, than I can escape from my diabetes or my emphysematous lung. My pancreas has not been all that it should be; nor has Moura. That does not alter the fact that both are parts of myself.

I have tried to set out my conclusions about all this love

business in the closing chapter of *The Anatomy of Frustration*, and I hope to insert a chapter upon "Promiscuity" in this book.[1] I have written *The Anatomy of Frustration* with sedulous care. Sometimes it seems to say all that I have to say, and sometimes I feel it is completely opaque.

The colour of life is largely a matter of homes. Thirteen Hanover Terrace will open a new phase, the last phase, of my life. Most of the furnishing is being arranged for me by my son Frank and his wife Peggy and Lady Colefax, but I have had a controlling voice in the arrangements, and I note that I have suddenly taken a vivid interest in installing a bust of Voltaire in my dining-room. It has seemed very important to me, and I perceive it symbolizes my vague anticipations of what this last chapter of my history may be; something after the fashion of Voltaire's contentment at Ferny. I intend, I realize, to be the old gentleman of Hanover Terrace, who, for a few years more, will still make his comments and suggestions to the end. I hope his brain will keep hard to the end. My father's did; my mother's did not.

We shall see.

The first of my films, *Things to Come*, was produced after a vast advertising campaign at the Leicester Square Cinema on February 21st, 1936. It had a considerable success from the commercial point of view, but for me it was a huge disillusionment. It was, I saw plainly, pretentious, clumsy and scamped. I had fumbled with it. My control of the production had been ineffective. Cameron Menzies was an incompetent director; he loved to get away on location and waste money on irrelevancies; and Korda let this happen. Menzies was a sort of Cecil B. de Mille without his imagination; his mind ran on

[1] He never wrote it. [G.P.W.]

loud machinery and crowd effects and he had no grasp of my ideas. He was sub-conscious of his own commonness of mind. He avoided every opportunity of talking to me. The most difficult part of this particular film, and the one most stimulating to the imagination, was the phase representing a hundred and twenty years hence, but the difficulties of the task of realization frightened Menzies; he would not get going on that, and he spent most of the available money on an immensely costly elaboration of the earlier two-thirds of the story. He either failed to produce, or he produced so badly that ultimately they had to cut out a good half of my dramatic scenes. Korda too disappointed me and above all I disappointed myself. I was taken by surprise by difficulties I should have foreseen. I did not take Korda's measure soon enough or secure an influence over him soon enough. I have called him congenial and he is—insinuatingly and untrustworthily congenial. I grew tired of writing stuff into the treatment that was afterwards mishandled or cut out again.

In the end little more of *The Shape of Things to Come* was got over than a spectacular suggestion of a Cosmopolis ruled by men of science and affairs. It presented, in the form of a World League of Airmen, the idea of the "New Beginning" as it is expounded in *The Anatomy of Frustration*. But though my disappointment with my first film enterprise was intense, and though I realized that, with just those half-educated people whose minds I wanted to influence, its noisy heaviness would damage my prestige, perhaps irreparably, it produced nothing like the depression and loss of hope that followed the frustration of my Moscow expedition. I was, I see, getting my mind in order through *The Anatomy of Frustration* and learning to take a defeat toughly.

The Man Who Could Work Miracles followed close on the heels of *Things to Come*. This was far more "producer-proof" than its predecessor. It was directed by Lothar Mendes, a far worse director even than Menzies; dull beyond words; it lost endless opportunities for sparkle and fun but it emerged a more coherent work of art altogether than its predecessor. I was still learning, I realized; I was growing; and this was a very pleasant realization in my seventieth year.

July 17th, 1936. I have not opened this "Looseleaf Diary" for a couple of months, but now I open it to add nothing but confirmatory material to what goes before. The new house is a success and I am physically and aesthetically happy in it. I have done myself well. I am working well. I have started a novel which amuses me in the old fashion, *The Show's the Thing* (a title afterwards changed to *Brynhild*), and I have opened a vigorous campaign in preparation for the launching of a modern encyclopaedia I shall certainly never live even to see it begun. Moura flits in and out after the old fashion. We have week-ended here and there, we gossip together and make love like husband and wife.

At the end of May 1936 a peculiar malaise came upon Moura. She had storms of weeping, a thing strangely unusual in her. She was seized with a desire to go off alone to France. The shadow of the coming change of life lay upon her. Her generally invincible self-assurance deserted her for a time. She couldn't talk to me about it; she couldn't talk to herself about that phase; she wanted to be alone. Then came something to pull her out of her depression. Suddenly the newspaper announced that Gorky was mortally ill in Moscow[2] and a few days afterwards I had a telegram from her in Russia. I do not think she had had any thought of going to Russia when she went to France, but abruptly she packed off to him. She helped nurse him; she saw him through his last delirium (which she described

[2] He died on June 19th, 1936. [G.P.W.]

to me); she did certain obscure things about his papers that she had promised to do for him long ago. I think there were documents that it was undesirable should fall into the hands of the Ogpu and that she secured them. I think there was something she knew and that she had promised to tell no one. And I believe that she kept her promise. In such matters Moura is invincibly sturdy. I shrugged my shoulders when she vanished out of my world, and was, I thought, prepared to go on living without her. I doubted the bona fides of Gorky in calling for her—quite unjustly. He had died so often before. Suppose now he just went on dying. What would she do?

I spent the three week-ends of Moura's absence; one with the Siegfried Sassoons in Wiltshire, a delightful couple; one with the Holdens in Sussex; and one over a queer international conference in London in which I did my best to kill a most undesirable project for a Marxist encyclopaedia. After that first telegram I heard no more from Moura and I thought that Russia had swallowed her up. I came back from the week-end at the Holdens on Sunday night and, about one o'clock in the morning, Moura, the incorrigible, unchangeable Moura, whom manifestly I love by nature and necessity, rang me up—as if she had never been away. . . .

It was as if she had come home.

This chapter returns into itself, *da capo*. I do not think there is going to be anything really fresh to tell about myself. The getting-on in life, the love story, the learning about the world, are all practically over. I am indifferent to death and tolerably reconciled to the prospect of old age. My life is settling down into a serenely active last phase. I like the setting of my life; this house in Hanover Terrace is pleasant in every way and the lines of my life are now almost continually agreeable. I do not feel lonely any more. I am interested in the films; in the forwarding at this point and at that point of the world community;

in the creation of an encyclopaedia of power; but I am interested as a man of science is interested in his work, as something greater than himself in which there is continual satisfaction and no end. My son Gip, my daughter-in-law Marjorie and one or two other people about me seem to have a similar philosophy and live in much the same spirit. I do not know how important my work may be from the viewpoint of the world. What matters to me is that it is important enough for me to carry me on.

I have said very little about my financial affairs. In these I have displayed an ordinary shrewdness and acquisitiveness, a certain not too detrimental slovenliness and an average honesty. I have done my best to evade income tax whenever I could safely do so without incurring anxiety, because I have thought it better, not only for myself but for my world, to live easily and work amply than to overtax myself for fools who build bombers and battleships and for the extravagances of incompetent administrators and officials.

(In 1938 I found myself in a situation when a compromise for arrears of income retained in America became necessary. Negotiations are still going on (February 1939) but I find this business, which may deprive me of half my capital, worries me very little. I have no sense of guilt at all in the matter. I have simply been careless and clumsy in my evasion. To which I add, in March 1939, that I settled the trouble with a payment of £23,000.)

The things for which I most reproach myself in life are mainly little acute things; tactlessness and irritability with my parents, my elder brother and people dependent upon me; making Jane unhappy at certain times and sometimes leaving her alone and uncomforted; humiliations I have inflicted—some like incurable little sores on my memory—pressure upon and actual cruelty to stupid small boys when I was a schoolmaster, killing a defenceless young rat with a walking-stick; fits of spiteful passion—for the most part innocuous. And sundry other such stupidities. I never get the slightest regret out of any of my sexual irregularities. They were amusing and refreshing and I wish there had been more of them. One remembers them as events that occurred but without any realist recollection of the details. It is like trying to recall the feeling of spring.

July 19th, 1936. So I close my *Autobiography*. I may live on yet for a dozen years or more, but I do not think it will be necessary to add a single essential thing more. I have exhausted my Self as a topic now, thank Heaven!, and I have told all that I have been able to make out of love. Moura and I will certainly stick together in our peculiar detached way. She will see to that if I don't. What remains will be work—and that will speak for itself—incidents—of no importance—and I suppose infirmities—of which the least said the better. It is no good meeting trouble half way.

Which conclusion I endorse on the eve of my seventieth birthday, September 21st, 1936—which (I add on October 6th) Moura and I celebrated very cheerfully together as we have celebrated it now for eight anniversaries.

I find I have not felt the autobiographical impulse for more than five months. Today is February 21st, 1937. Nothing essential has happened to me. Thirteen Hanover Terrace continues to be a successful home and I have not wanted to leave it for ten months. London University made me a Doctor of Literature at its centenary and I was secretly annoyed because it was not a doctorate of science. I was given a big public dinner by my absurd P.E.N. Club on October 13th, and so much stress was laid upon my Seventy Years that for a time I really felt the burthen of them. And I have had all my remaining teeth out and at the time that mortified me greatly. But I seem to be recovering my elasticity. I have finished and polished up what I think is a fairly satisfactory short novel, *Brynhild*, and two long-short stories which really please me, *The Croquet Player*, already published in book form, and *Star-Begotten. The Croquet Player* has succeeded with the press and the booksellers. I dedicated it to Moura. In addition I have agreed to be President of the Education Section of the British Association meeting at Nottingham in September and my address is already written. Moreover I have written a lecture which I shall deliver in October in America, on the topic of the World Encyclopaedia. That idea grows in importance in my mind; it is full of creative possibility. The trend of thought in these two addresses, in *Star-Begotten* and in *The Anatomy of Frustration*, is all in the same direction. It arises in due order out of *The Shape of Things to Come*. I am getting a sort of stereoscopic vision of the future; it becomes more real and solid with each new slant of approach. I believe that the system of ideas I am developing is one likely to have much more influence upon the world than is apparent at the present time. The idea of a World Encyclopaedia crowns the arch of the Competent Receiver and the Open Conspiracy.

No doubt all this work of mine might have been planned better and better written; it might have been advanced more convincingly and have produced a more immediate effect, but that does not distress me. It had to grow in its own fashion; it could not be planned ahead. Seeing what I am, I think I have done fairly well with myself. I am past the age of exalted ambitions, disappointments and self-reproach. I am what I am and I know my plan and scale. And Moura remains what she is; rather stouter, rather greyer, sometimes tiresome, oftener charming and close and dear.

In the last week or so I have turned back to a story I began long ago, *Dolores and Happiness*. It turns away from my world preoccupation towards what I may call the humour of life. In a way it is myself, *en pantoufles*. I shall play about with it and take no steps for its publication.

On July 9th, 1937, I glance at this manuscript, but there is little to add. I have had a severe attack of neuritis which has incapacitated me for a couple of months and now I am better. The spell of neuritis was a depressing experience while it lasted, but the recovery had an air of victory about it, and it is pleasant to recover and find my working power is not over, and that I have reserves of strength. I was in my bathroom feeling very unsound, and I stubbed my toe, and, let me confess it, I whimpered with self-pity. And then I gave way to anger and self-disgust. Instead of getting into my nice warm bath, I ran it out and stood up under the cold douche Let it be real pain, I said. I got rid of all my pain cures and went on as if I had no neuritis at all. And behold! I had no neuritis. Either I had recovered just then or I had done the right thing to cure myself of this ache of the nerves. So far as I can understand it was caused by a deficiency of Vitamin B_2 due to too strict a diabetic dietary.

But I am growing old—manifestly, so far as my body goes. Mentally, I am still active. I have finished a third long-short story, *The Brothers*, I have thrown off a fourth fantasy, an attack on the pettiness of our university objectives, *The Camford Visitation*, and I am going on again with *Dolores and Happiness*, the title of which I have changed to *Happiness and the Evil Heart* (*Light Heart, Evil Heart*, August 30th, 1937, and ultimately to *Apropos of Dolores*, February 1938). It is an amusing novel, I think, and I am drawing on the character of Odette with some freedom—and I do not think with very great malice.

I mean this to be a very leisurely, discursive novel on which I will work when it pleases me for the next year or so. (And now in March 1938 it is done!)

I find I draw closer to my family than I did and like them all more and more. In their varied ways they are a good bunch. Moura and I see each other nearly every day when we are both in England and are very content in an amused and tolerant way with each other. The world is a world of disorder and menace, but there is nothing for it but to go on as steadfastly as possible with this quite possibly futile working-out of the new order which I have made the framework of my life.

In September 1937 I was President of the Educational Section of the British Association at Nottingham. I made it the occasion of a vigorous attack upon the poorness of the informative side of contemporary schoolteaching and there were some lively discussions. The presidential address with a diagram is in my little book *World Brain*.

I add on November 28th, 1937, that I have been to America and returned. I have found it stimulating and I return stronger and more energetic than I went. I have given the World Encyclopaedia project a push, but just what this push amounts to I cannot estimate. The impressions of that trip are given in an article *Fall in America 1937*, which is reprinted in *World Brain*, with my various lectures and essays on this subject. I am back at the old life here in Hanover Terrace with everything, Moura and all, going smoothly along the established lines.

And now (April 4th, 1938) in an unusually early and delightful spring, I note a steady stabilization of my health and that I am revising the last chapters of my *Short History* and beginning a new and I think very promising novel about a very human and possible Dictator, *The Holy Terror*. And Moura is Moura as ever; human, faulty, wise, silly, and I love her.

Our world has passed into a phase of extreme war-apprehension and preparation and a great financial slump, affecting the business and property of almost everyone unpleasantly, is going on throughout the world. Naturally these shadows fall upon Moura and myself directly and indirectly. We are much more anxious for our various children and for many of our friends than for ourselves, for we have in common a certain adventurous stoicism. I see my conception of a world-state recede—recede but not disappear—and decades of tragic futility and confusion that I had not foreseen, had not been willing to foresee, become more and more probable. But there is nothing for it for me but to carry on with the problems of the world-state. That has to be worked out by persistent men, by many persistent men. No jerry-built emergency solutions can shorten that steady elaboration of the rational conception of life. Moura and I have little disposition for self-preservation from the physical dangers and mental stresses that seem to be coming nearer. We shall live according to our several lights, with different idea systems but a common temperamental quality, and we shall continue to be a great comfort to each other. We shall not be engulfed by the situation. We will not subdue ourselves to war service or to mere pacificist activities. We may be destroyed, but until then we shall carry on and be ourselves. In the long run the world order will come and maybe then some friendly reader will turn over these pages and wonder why we in our time could ever doubt its coming.

On November 28th, 1938, I add that I am packing my bag to go as one of five guests to the meeting of the Australia and New Zealand Association for the Advancement of Science at Canberra. I shall go by air to Marseilles, then by sea to Fremantle, then by air and car to Canberra and home *via* Sydney, Bali, Batavia, Medan, Rangoon, Jodhpur, Baghdad, and Athens. I am looking forward to three weeks' warmth and rest in the Indian Ocean. I shall return to Athens where Moura will meet me and spend a week or so in Greece before I come home.

The war crisis has passed through some astonishing phases. I have found it mentally stimulating and I have produced a number of articles and radio talks about it. More and more do I realize the need of a vigorous educational renascence based on the idea of a world order to save the human situation. The history on which we shape our political conduct becomes more and more manifestly the falsified record of a series of bloody messes. Man has never yet got a grip upon his destiny and he still has to achieve that. I drum away at this idea, in a score of different forms. I begin to feel old in many small ways; I can walk less actively; smoke, eat and drink less; but, so far, I don't detect much failure in my thinking and writing and in the liveliness of my intellectual interests. *Apropos of Dolores* has had some very appreciative reviews and *The Holy Terror* has excited various editors, publishers and so forth as much as anything I have done for some time.

November 30th, 1938. I have had two rather interesting conversations in the past week. One was with Benes, the fallen President of Czechoslovakia. I had met him in June in Prague while he was still in the Hradschin Palace, and then, in spite of the political crisis then impending, we had talked chiefly of the relative prospects of Russian and German as the cultural language for South-Eastern Europe. I was in Prague with the P.E.N. Club. Benes and I had met before during the Presidency of Masaryk, and I think he found my point of view stimulating. In a few weeks he was bawled out of Prague by Hitler (supported by that intolerable fool, Chamberlain) and he came to London. For a time he would see nobody, and then he told Jan Masaryk, who was still in the Czech Legation, that he would like to see me. I found him in complete agreement with the interpretation I have put upon the War Panic of the autumn, an interpretation I have embodied in a New Year's article for the *Cosmopolitan* and the *News Chronicle*. We talked about the general philosophy of life, and I explained the Mystical Stoicism into which I am settling down; as I have explained in the closing chapter of *The Holy Terror* and the latter part of *Apropos of Dolores*. It appealed to him and it appealed also to Freud, to whom I went to say goodbye yesterday. He was cheerful, rather wickedly excited about the book he has prepared about Moses and the origins of religion, and doing his best to talk in spite of the decay of his lower jaw. He was disposed to argue that a fully adult human being has no religion. I on the other hand held that I was fully adult and an essentially religious person. In effect we were in entire agreement. We hate the creeping enfeeblement that is overtaking us, but if that could be arrested we would like to go on for another fifty years. We hate burying our brains until we have used them up. Moura came in to fetch me away. She had met him first with me when we were in Vienna in the Dollfuss time. It was interesting to see him light up at the sight of her. Someone had given him some camellias and he decorated her with one. I suppose, if we go on to a hundred, men of our type will brighten up at a smiling woman.

May 25th, 1939, finds me at the end of another book, *The Fate of Homo sapiens*. This time I feel I have really said what I have had in me to say.

Since I made my last entry I have been to Canberra and back by air, visiting Bali, Rangoon, Jodhpur and Athens on the way. Moura was waiting for me at Athens and we visited Sunium and Delphi together. I stood the journey very well, but in Baghdad I picked up a germ that presently, after three weeks' incubation, broke out as shingles and left me with a spastic colon to get the better of. I broke out into a series of bitter and contemptuous articles in the *News Chronicle* until one about the Royal Family was altogether too much for the editor. Then I concentrated upon *The Fate of Homo sapiens*. And now I have done it, and of what I shall do next I have not the slightest idea.

On September 1st, 1940, I reopen this folder. I think I have told my story completely, and done with myself in the narrower sense altogether. There is little to add except an increased and livelier affection for my family and a generalization of my intellectual life. It is as if I have had a phase of shrinking back into myself since first I began the *Autobiography*, and that now I am escaping from that preoccupation. These changes may be normal changes in the life-cycle, or they may mark phases of ill-health and readjustment in my individual body. Moreover by writing all this autobiographical matter I think I have assured myself against the dangers of posthumous misrepresentation, which I have had considerable reason to fear. That again is a release from self. I am planning to go lecturing in America this autumn and return by Christmas.

This time last year I was in Sweden at the house of Huebsch the publisher at Flens, between Gothenburg and Stockholm, trying to hold together a P.E.N. Conference in the face of the breaking war-storm. Moura, who had been in Estonia for a few weeks, joined me at Flens. We were in Stockholm when war was declared on Germany on September 3rd, 1939. I have given a glimpse of the Stockholm atmosphere in *Babes in the Darkling Wood*. We had some little difficulty in getting by air to Amsterdam, and there we stuck for a tedious week until we got a passage on the last boat to go to England. We passed a convoy coming out of the Thames and we saw the last of the aircraft-carrier *Courageous* which was torpedoed that night.

The war stimulated my mind very greatly, and it did very much to assist in the *diminuendo* of my personal life. My story becomes my books and newspaper articles and controversial writings, *The Fate of Homo sapiens*, *The New World Order*, certain "Penguin Specials"—namely, *Travels of a Republican Radical in Search of Hot Water*, *The Rights of Man* and *The Commonsense of War and Peace*—my *Babes in the Darkling Wood* and a blasphemous lark, *All Aboard for Ararat*. These have been the essence of my life during this swift latest twelvemonth.

In September 1940, on my birthday—which had therefore to be celebrated overnight—I went aboard the Cunarder *Scythia* at Liverpool, and, after three nights of vigorous bombing while we waited for a convoy, we went off to New York. (Moura came as far as Liverpool and got back to London before the raids began.) There I stayed for a week or so with the Lamonts and then handed myself over to Peat, my agent. I lectured thirteen times, the same lecture which I polished continually, mainly on the abolition of distance—my title was "Two Hemispheres or One World"—and the necessity of America, the British states and Russia getting together upon a common understanding about the peace of the world. I was nearly a year ahead in my insistence on that, and we had some brisk discussion with the audience after the final lecture. America at that time was stupidly and ignorantly anti-Bolshevik and sentimentally but still rather ineffectively pro-British. I flew all over the States, doing over 24,000 miles by air.

I stood the journey and the work very well. Peat is a wonderful agent; he combines the duties of a batman with the wisdom of a skilled impresario. Wherever he goes, accommodating young ladies appear at his call, and he is mindful of the needs of his client. I had what I think should be a last flare of cheerful sensuality. I loved it, but there is nothing to be told about it. I went from New York to San Francisco and from the snows of Connecticut to the sunny lawns of Florida, Denver and Dallas, Birmingham and Detroit, Texas and Toledo, saying over my piece and writing much that I subsequently incorporated in my *Guide to the New World.* I had a rough and tedious journey home and stood it well. The Pan-American Airways took me to Bermuda and dropped me there in favour of mailbags for which the organization had a priority contract. I basked in Bermuda and then came on by the *Excalibur* to Lisbon, and so, after some days of delay, home, on January 4th, 1941. Since when I have done all sorts of things, but chiefly what I have tried to make my best and most comprehensive novel, *You Can't be Too Careful*. I sent that to Warburg the day before yesterday, August 10th, 1941. (And it was published on December 16th, belatedly because of the paper famine, the shortage of skilled binders and so forth.)

I bring this story down to the moment of writing this note, Christmas 1941. From the bombings in the spring of 1940, the war went on confirming my forecasts at a constantly accelerated speed. I wrote a number of articles of bitter remonstrance at the conduct of the war, but gradually the spirit of censorship restricted my outlets and it was plain I could affect the immediate course of events only very slightly. It seemed that the best thing to do was to set down certain things so plainly and exactly that, if the staggering world did presently righten itself, there they would be, available for kindred spirits to start upon. I rewrote that little out-of-date book of mine, *First and Last Things*; I induced a number of intelligent people to read over the new version and criticize it and discuss it with me, and when I got it as hard and polished as I could, I replaced *First and Last Things* in the Rationalist Press Association's lists by what I am calling *The Conquest of Time*. At the same time I am putting all I know about the history of warfare into a compact, but very meaty, little book, which I shall call *A Baiting of Warriors*. This ought to be in print by June 1942. It stands by itself but I think it may light up a number of young people about the elements of the war-problem.

A third book, which is already in the press, is a concentration of a number of current affairs books and articles that I have published in the past two years, *The Fate of Homo sapiens*, *The New World Order*, *Guide to the New World*, *The Commonsense of War and Peace*. These books go out; they must be read here and there. It is impossible to estimate their effect. The new concentration is to be called *The Outlook for Homo sapiens*, and Warburg will release it early in 1942. I have also given a drastic revision of the old *Outline of History*, the stocks of which in this country were destroyed when Cassell's were bombed.

The Japanese attack has revealed the immense unimaginative incompetence and indolence of the dominant people in both America and Great Britain. Neither army nor navy betrays any sense of co-operation; after Crete, Japan, Burma, they still do not understand the elementary need of establishing air-fields as part of their raids and of sticking to every foothold they gain. They make their silly hit-and-run "on commando" expeditions—why the bloody fools have raked up this South African Boy Scout word for the plain English word "raid" only the God of fools can explain—alas, it was Winston in one of his feebler moments!—and having induced the local people to rise in the bright hope that here was at last a bona fide raid, off they go again leaving the poor devils who have trusted the seriousness of their intentions to be shot by the hundred. Now instead of preparing raids in close co-operation with the local support, as I demanded a year and a half ago, they seem bent on repeating the foolery of 1941 by sending miscellaneous token forces unused to any co-operation to practically certain disaster. They are going to muck it up—they could not muck it up more if they planned to muck it up. One cannot stop this sort of thing. This fool's "British Empire" has to be cleared away and the sooner it goes, I suppose, the better. But I am English; all I care for in my blood and bones is involved in this spectacular disaster, and what is happening tears me to pieces.

The tempo of events has increased beyond all my expectations. We shall get through something analogous to the Dark Ages in a few decades. But even if we have decades for centuries I doubt if I shall last out to see the new phase of world unity detach itself from the collapse of the past. I doubt if I shall live to see the end of this silly monarchy; this lying religious organization; this foul educational swindle; this tangle of snobbery and overreaching; that has been my inescapable background.

I have jeered at it; I have laughed at it; maybe I have done something to hasten its end. I think if I write any more I shall have to write a book called *Reconstruction*, a sort of assembly and criticism of hopes and projects. I must think that over. . . .

(And here in April 1942 I have thought it over. I have had a series of rapid realizations, coming very fast one after the other—I have tried to make their sequence clear in the end chapters of the first volume of *Phoenix*, the happy title invented by Moura for this crowning book. Now I am living a life of almost intolerable impatience lest some unforeseen obstacle should hold up this most urgent and conclusive work. I cannot endure these dragging days and at times I come near to the screaming pitch.)

There is little to add about Moura. She is fifty now. It is twenty years since our first intimacy. Then she was a tall and slender young woman and now I told her she was like a Vatican cherub, three times life-size but still delightful, an ample woman; she is very grey but that queer sub-dropsy that attacks so many women of her age, and thickens their ankles, has spared hers altogether.

I wrote that at Christmas 1941 but since then life has taken on a still grimmer visage (April 1942). Something very bitter, I cannot tell the ugly particulars now, has hurt her heartbreakingly—in her pride and in her affections. Thank the Fates there is something incurably childish in her make-up. She can forget utter disaster in the surprise of an unexpected bottle of wine or a glowing fire. I cannot do it like that. I have seen the world catastrophe creep nearer and engulf things that were very dear to me. I am distressed at the ugly things that may happen to my grandchildren and which I cannot avert. And though I have suffered no great physical injuries I feel that I would now gradually turn my face to the wall for good and give up this last instalment of my life. I have lived out my essential career. Oldish people nowadays go to bed and ebb out from existence in the devitalizing small hours. Heart-failure is the diagnosis. That seems to me now to be an enviable release.

Death is one of the best things that have happened to life. It is not a primordial thing. For a long way up the scale of existence there are such things as conjugation, rejuvenescence, fission; but there is no dying. It is only with the appearance of detached individuals who go out into the world, struggle for life, are accepted or rejected, altering or failing to alter the species, that death comes as the crown and definition of life. The individual fights stoutly to live on, and the stouter the individual the more it has accumulated a surplus of energy beyond the bare minimum needed to survive. So that even when, as in this present hour of world collapse, distress and bitter disillusionment overtake us all and existence is less and less acceptable, it is still against habit and instinct to die.

Stefan Zweig committed a deliberate suicide because he felt there was nothing more for him to do in the world. All his effective contacts had been broken. He felt a useless exile. I think him completely justified, but I know there is work and urgent and important work I may presently be called upon to do, and that I cannot go like that. I am here with all my books and a loyal household at hand.

A young mind is like a green field and full of possibilities, but an old mind becomes more and more like a cemetery crowded up with memories. There may be an accumulation of knowledge, counsel and critical power, but only if the mind has never let go of life. Once that is done I doubt if we can pick it up again. I claim to be an exceptional case of holding on and holding out and I have to justify that claim.

Presently I suppose I shall have to recover—when *Phoenix* is fairly launched my last sound excuse will have gone for malingering—but for the time I have turned my face to the wall and I am resolved to keep my face turned to the wall just as long as I possibly can. And lying with my face to the wall in this recalcitrant mood I have made some very definite resolutions. And the first is to make an end with bores. There is no reason now why I should ever be bored again.

Why should I? My job of rebellion, which began when I was born, is now fully achieved and done. My mother's diary records that I squalled with extreme violence at the font. I would like to imagine I struck at the parson with my puny fist, but there is no proper evidence for that. My mute demand, "What is this lie of a world you have brought me into?" has taken me nearly seventy-six years to answer, but at last I have got the answer clear and plain. So far no one in the whole world has sustained so long an effort and brought it to such completion, and now I can sweep aside a thousand petty disputes and persuasions as a chemical investigator sweeps aside the trial experiments that led to his ultimate discovery. There is this book, *Phoenix*. It is written with vehement plainness. If you cannot understand it, read it again or quibble away from it, but anyhow do not pester me.

Beside *Phoenix* is my clear, carefully elaborated statement of how mankind stands in the scheme of things, *You Can't be Too Careful*. That tells you as ruthlessly and explicitly as possible the reality about the contemporary human animal, of myself and yourself and the species. You can protest that you are altogether nobler, wiser, more beautiful within and without than Edward Albert Tewler. I will not argue with you. Anything you can say or do I shall disregard entirely. I have said my ultimate say. You are completely and finally answered and all your possible Tewlerisms are dealt with in that book. Read it again but don't bother me. You will never get nearer to me now than the waste-paper basket (April 28th, 1942).

§2
Note by another hand

Here it is that another hand should take up the story for me and fill in a few particulars at which I can only guess. My alleged prophetic power fails me. I guess and hope it will be heart failure in the night—with all my affairs in order.

"H. G. Wells died ..." this section should run....

Those lines he wrote himself. The rest is by his eldest son.

... on August 13th, 1946, a month before his eightieth birthday. In his last years he was increasingly ill and increasingly helpless—not so much in pain as weak—and for more than two of them he was tactfully watched and helped by nurses, day and night. He refused to leave London and these years were spent in his house at Hanover Terrace, among (except for a few months at the end) the exploding bombs and V-weapons of World War II. Moura was in and out of the house and he was visited by many old friends.

There were other books after *Phoenix*. *Crux Ansata*, a polemical work attacking the Roman Catholic Church, came in 1943 and *'42 to '44* a year later. That was a collection of essays on various subjects, including a thesis which he had submitted, successfully, for the Doctorate of Science of a rather puzzled University of London, in 1944. In the same year he sent to press his last revision of the *Short History of the World*, to which he added a concluding chapter, titled "Mind at the End of its Tether," surprising his readers with the announcement that there was no future for mankind. *Homo sapiens* must follow the dinosaurs to extinction.

Why did he reach this conclusion? Because he had insisted,

over and over again, that man, if he wishes to survive, must consciously adapt his thinking and his way of life to the new environment his cleverness has made. He must "adapt or perish." And, especially, he must eliminate war by setting up a supernational World-State, or Union of States, for the preservation of peace. To be effective, this authority must, of course, have power to define and limit the armaments of every country in the world, and every country must surrender to it a considerable measure of independence.

In the closing chapters of *Experiment in Autobiography* my father tells how, during World War I, he and others who felt as he did pressed for the setting up of a Federal World-State as its outcome. But instead there was set up a League of independent sovereign Nations directed by a Council of nine whose decisions had to be unanimous—one dissentient could veto any proposal. In my father's words, "a complete recognition of the unalienable sovereignty of states, and a repudiation of the idea of an overriding commonwealth of mankind."

Still he fought on, to the best of his ebbing powers, as the war-clouds gathered and darkened again, to break in 1939.

The last of his many revisions of *The Outline of History* was completed near the end of 1940,[1] when Britain was fighting Germany and Italy, France was beaten and occupied, and Japan's aggression was confined as yet to Chiang Kai-shek's China. Russia and America were still technically neutral and this encouraged him to think it just possible that the world might emerge from World War II into a Federated World-State, "provided America and Russia could agree about it." The war need not be won or lost. Better neither. The two giant powers, preserving their neutrality, could jointly plan the

[1] *The Enlarged and Revised Outline of History*, Garden City Publishing Co. Inc., copyright 1940. Owing to wartime conditions this revision was never published in the United Kingdom.

terms of an Armistice setting up a world organization, "federal and international in the full sense of the word ... not made up of contingents from the separate powers" and "the combatant states, as they approach exhaustion and entire disorganization, could be invited to accept them.... This is no Utopian dream; it is the plain commonsense of what has to be done now. It is as plain a necessity as ploughing and sowing and making clothes.... No sort of lesser peace is now possible that would be anything better than a resting-place between hostilities. Sooner or later, therefore, the Armistice must come, or mankind must blunder down through unending warfare to destruction."

In January 1941 he returned from a lecture tour of America where he had put forward these ideas (p. 224). But it soon became clear that a Federal World Organization was not to be. The two great neutrals were brought into the war as combatants by the German invasion of Russia in June 1941 and the surprise Japanese attack on Pearl Harbor in December of the same year. Germany and Japan surrendered four years later and the victors met at San Francisco to replace the League by the United Nations, once again an organization "made up of contingents from the separate powers." On the central Security Council of eleven, any one of the five Permanent Members could veto, without reason given, decisions made by the majority. So there was division instead of federation, and the world watched the start of an arms race with weapons of unprecedented ingenuity and deadliness.

It was, I believe, his realization of the way things were going that led to *Mind at the End of Its Tether*, as it led to the bitterness of the last entries in his "Looseleaf Diary." "Humanity cannot remain where it is; it cannot stay at its present level.... If man does not go steeply downwards in the eventful decades ahead of us it will be because he has at last developed the wits to go steeply upward." Thus he had written in the 1940 *Outline of History*, and it now seemed to him that man was incapable of going upward. Incapable, that is, of survival.

Not that he stopped working, or denied himself an occasional flicker of irrational hope. In 1945 there appeared several articles and his last two books—a sombre expansion of *Mind at the End of Its Tether* and a cheerful suite of allegories and dreams called *The Happy Turning.*[2]

His final publication was an article in the *New Leader* for July 1946, fiercely attacking "all the unteachable elderly, all the conservative elements in our intricate and confused national life." It appeared less than six weeks before his heart stopped beating—not, as he guessed, in the night but in the afternoon. His worldly affairs, thanks to his secretary, who was also my wife, were in reasonably good order.

G. P. W.

[2] The two are reprinted, with an account by myself of his last years, in *The Last Books of H. G. Wells*, published by the H. G. Wells Society.

§3
About the Publication of this Postscript[1]

I do not know if this Postscript to my Autobiography will ever be published. I want it to be published as soon as that can conveniently be done, but whether my heirs will see to that and whether sufficient interest in my life will survive to justify that is quite beyond my powers of anticipation. Copies of it may be typed as family documents for the private reading of my children; I want them to know all about me. (It is very doubtful what will happen to book publishing and reading in the years ahead. It may be a perfectly practical proposition to document H. G. Wells as fully as I am going to suggest or it may be a fantastic impossibility in a stressed, under-educated and impoverished world.) *If it should seem* (practicable and) *worth while a few years after my death*, when ***** and Moura and Dusa are either dead or consenting—for Odette does not matter a rap; Rebecca, bless her, is fully able to take care of herself; ***** won't mind,[2] and nobody else has any justification for complaint—if then it should seem worth while *so to round off my attempted self-portrait of*

[1] The original text of this note, written early in 1935, is printed here in italics. Subsequent additions are in roman. Most of the inserted matter was added at various times in the eighteen months to autumn 1936—a period during which the whole of the *Postscript* was being repeatedly worked over and revised as explained above (pp. 17–18). Then came a three-year lull and after that a few more additions, shown here in brackets, were made. It will be seen that the requirement "not by itself" was included in the original draft and vigorously endorsed several years later, in 1939/40, by the addition of "I underline that."

Names deleted from the main text in this edition are here replaced by asterisks. [G. P. W.]

[2] She did. [G. P. W.]

a brain in this age of the opening conflict between the new big-scale life and (human egotism, disconnectedness and) *the little life of tradition, then I hope that it may be possible to publish this "Postscript"—not by itself* (I underline that) *but bound up with the rest of my Autobiography and with the preface I wrote to "The Book of Catherine Wells." "Experiment in Autobiography," the preface to "The Book of Catherine Wells" and this "Postscript" should follow one after the other. So all the main masses of my experiences and reactions will fall into proportion.* Neither is complete without the other, but together they make a fairly stereoscopic self-portrait of as much of a mind as could force itself to confession in this age of transition. As I have intimated already, I have flinched at one or two minor things—misdeeds for the most part of no extensive significance—indignities I did myself.

(I cannot imagine that the world will ever stand a complete posthumous edition of my works, but I like to brood on so much survival, and if so I think all this autobiographical stuff should come at the end of the rest.)

I hope no subsequent editor will be disposed to cut down the main Autobiography because the science or the philosophy or the references to political conditions may seem to have fallen out of date or have become a little difficult to understand. Let them be annotated if need be, but they are History and the rest of my personal adventure cannot be properly understood without them—nor they without the rest of my experiences. *The directive idea of my life, even if it had to draw its driving force from the imperfect sublimation of my intimate impulses, was the creative World-State*—which in its individual aspect is the candid, co-operative, creative World-Man.

I am English by origin but I am an early World-Man and I live in exile from the world community of my desires. I salute that finer larger world and its subtler minds across the generations—and maybe ever again someone down the vista, some lingering vestige of my Lover-Shadow, may look back and appreciate an ancestral salutation.

§4
NOTE ON FATE AND INDIVIDUALITY[1]

As I turn over the pages of this manuscript I shall never see in print I find another thought floating beside me, that I do not want to stress but which, because it is a qualifying reflection, I ought not to discard altogether.

It is impossible, I find, to write autobiography with as much sincerity as I have sought, telling of limitations, frustrations, intrinsic failure and accepted defeats, without the picture beginning to take on more and more the quality of a fated destiny, without feeling more and more plainly how close one's experiences have come to those of a creature of innate impulses, caught by circumstances and making an ineffectual buzzing about it like a fly on a fly-paper. That floating thought, in short, is predestination. This story, apparently of a character and a will, is really the trace of the reaction between internal and external forces, equally destined and rigid. I have indeed not written an autobiography, but merely made a brief inadequate sketch of my life, a *trace*, "as it was written from the beginning."

This is an aspect of life that my militant instinct has always been disposed to ignore and against which every active factor in me shouts "No!" But something fundamental will have

[1]Written early in 1935 to conclude the "Postscript," this "Note" survived all of the subsequent revisions virtually unchanged and was still present as the peroration in the final typescript. But my father had drawn a pencil line through it, both in the contents table and in the text of that last typescript, so he may have wished to exclude it for some reason. Meanwhile, almost the whole of this "Note" was put into the mouth of the mythical Steele in *The Anatomy of Frustration* (published 1936; see p. 17 above). [G.P.W.]

been withheld from the reality of the whole; there will be less of a solidity, a flatness, if I do not recognize the presence of this aspect in my mind. And also it is present in my mind that some flies (a little sticky perhaps and hampered) do somehow get away from the fly-paper of circumstance.

I am left in the end with an unconquered sense of my own individuality as significant—as primary. My last words about this Self I have been ransacking are this, that this creature *has had, has and transmits free will.* Not much free will, not much courage or assertion, but some. More than the fly on the fly-paper has. An increasing amount. And free will *is* individuality, and individuality is nothing else. Individuality is intrinsic uniqueness and spontaneous initiative. Spontaneous initiative is creation and creation is divinity. And that, I realize, is what I began to say in my first published article, *The Rediscovery of the Unique*, in the *Fortnightly Review* of July 1891, written at Up Park, Petersfield, forty-five years ago (1936).

CHRONOLOGY

1866	Born 21 September, Bromley, Kent. His mother a lady's maid, later a housekeeper; his father a gardener, later a cricketer and shopkeeper
1874–9	Morley's Commercial Academy, Bromley
1880	Apprenticed to Rodgers and Denyer, drapers, Windsor
1881	With Samuel Cowap, chemist, Midhurst, Sussex (one month); Hyde's Drapery Emporium, Southsea (two years' apprenticeship)
1883–4	Midhurst Grammar School (teaching scholar)
1884	The Normal School (later Royal College) of Science, South Kensington
1886	Matriculated, London University
1887	Taught at the Holt Academy, Wrexham, North Wales
1889	Henley House School, Kilburn, London
1890–3	University Correspondence College (tutor)
1890	B.Sc. London University (First-Class in zoology, Second in geology)
1891	Married his cousin Isabel Mary Wells. "The Rediscovery of the Unique" in *Fortnightly Review*
1893	Left his wife for Amy Catherine Robbins, one of his students. *Textbook of Biology. Honours Physiography* (with R. A. Gregory)
1895	Divorced. Married Amy Catherine Robbins. Published *Select Conversations With an Uncle*, *The Time Machine*, *The Stolen Bacillus*, *The Wonderful Visit*

NOTE: This chronology has been compiled by the publishers for the convenience of readers.

1896	"Human Evolution: An Artificial Process" (*Fortnightly Review*), *The Island of Dr. Moreau*, *The Wheels of Chance*
1897	"Morals and Civilisation" (*Fortnightly Review*), *The Plattner Story*, *The Invisible Man*, *Certain Personal Matters*, *Thirty Strange Stories*, *The Star*
1898	*The War of the Worlds*
1899–1900	Spade House built at Sandgate, Kent; architect C.F.A. Voysey. *When the Sleeper Wakes*, *Tales of Space and Time*
1900	*Love and Mr. Lewisham*
1901	George Philip Wells born. *The First Men in the Moon*, *Anticipations*, *A Dream of Armageddon*
1902	*The Discovery of the Future* (Royal Institution lecture), *The Sea Lady*
1903	Frank Richard Wells born. Joined the Fabian Society. *Mankind in the Making*, *The Food of the Gods*. *Twelve Stories and a Dream*, "The Land Ironclads" (tank story, *Strand Magazine*)
1904	*The Food of the Gods*
1905	*Kipps: The Story of a Simple Soul*, *A Modern Utopia*
1906	First visit to America. *In the Days of the Comet*, *Faults of the Fabian*, *The Future in America*, *Socialism and the Family*
1907	*This Misery of Boots* (Fabian Society), *The So-Called Science of Sociology*
1908	Resigned from the Fabian Society. *First and Last Things*, *New Worlds for Old*, *The War in the Air*
1909	Moved to London from Sandgate. *Tono-Bungay*, *Ann Veronica: A Modern Love Story*
1910	*The History of Mr. Polly*
1911	*The New Machiavelli*, *The Country of the Blind and Other Stories*, *Floor Games* (for children)
1912	Moved to Easton Glebe, Essex, but also kept a

	flat in London. *Marriage,* "The Past and the Great State" in *The Great State: Essays in Construction*
1913	*The Passionate Friends, Little Wars*
1914	Anthony West born. *The War That Will End War, An Englishman Looks at the World, The World Set Free, The Wife of Sir Isaac Harman*
1915	*Boon* (under the pseudonym Reginald Bliss), *The Research Magnificent, Bealby*
1916	Visited the Italian, French and German war fronts. *The Elements of Reconstruction, What is Coming?, Mr. Britling Sees It Through*
1917	*War and the Future, God the Invisible King, The Soul of a Bishop*
1918	Prepared anti-German material for Lord Northcliffe's Ministry of Propaganda. *In the Fourth Year* (including "A Reasonable Man's Peace"), *Joan and Peter*
1919	Part author of *The Idea of a League of Nations. History is One, The Undying Fire*
1920	Met Lenin in Moscow. *The Outline of History, Russia in the Shadows*
1921	*The Salvaging of Civilisation.* Washington Conference
1922	Contested London University parliamentary seat as official Labour candidate without success. Tried again in 1923. Defeated by Lord Birkenhead in election for Rectorship of Glasgow University. *A Short History of the World, The Secret Places of the Heart, Washington and the Hope of Peace*
1923	*Socialism and the Scientific Motive, Men Like Gods*
1924	Houses on the French Riviera (Lou Bastidon near Grasse, later Lou Pidou). *A Year of Prophesying, The Dream, The Story of a Great Schoolmaster*

1925 *Christina Alberta's Father*

1926 *The World of William Clissold*, *Mr. Belloc Objects to the Outline of History*

1927 Death of Catherine Wells. *The Complete Short Stories*, *Meanwhile*, *Democracy Under Revision* (Sorbonne lecture)

1928 *The Book of Catherine Wells* ("Introduction" by H.G.W.), *The Open Conspiracy*, *The Way the World is Going*, *Mr. Blettsworthy on Rampole Island*

1929 *The Common Sense of World Peace* (address to the Reichstag in Berlin), *The King Who Was a King* (film script), *The Adventures of Tommy* (for children)

1930 *The Science of Life* (with Julian Huxley and G. P. Wells), Easton Glebe sold. *The Autocracy of Mr. Parham*

1931 *What Are We to Do With Our Lives?*, *The Work, Wealth and Happiness of Mankind*

1932 *After Democracy*, *The Bulpington of Blup*

1933 *The Shape of Things to Come*

1934 To Moscow to talk with Stalin. *Experiment in Autobiography*

1935 Bought 13 Hanover Terrace. Wrote about the New Deal in America. Met F. D. Roosevelt. *The New America*. *Things to Come* (film script)

1936 Hon. D.Lit., London University. *The Anatomy of Frustration*, *The Man Who Could Work Miracles* (film script), *The Croquet Player*, *The Idea of a World Encyclopædia*

1937 "My Obituary" in *Coronet* magazine. *The Camford Visitation*, *Star-Begotten*, *Brynhild*

1938 *World Brain*, *The Brothers*, *Apropos of Dolores*

1939 In Stockholm when war was declared. *The Fate of Homo sapiens*, *Travels of a Republican Radical in*

	Search of Hot Water, The Holy Terror
1940	*The Rights of Man, The Commonsense of War and Peace, All Aboard for Ararat, Babes in the Darkling Wood, The New World Order.* Last visit to the United States
1941	*Guide to the New World, You Can't be Too Careful: A Sample of Life 1901–51*
1942	*The Outlook for Homo sapiens, Science and the World Mind, The Conquest of Time, Phoenix: A Summary of the Inescapable Conditions of World Organisation*
1943	*Crux Ansata: An Indictment of the Roman Catholic Church*
1944	Awarded D.Sc. by University of London for his *Thesis on the Quality of Illusion in the Continuity of the Individual Life in the Higher Metazoa, with Particular Reference to the Species Homo Sapiens. '42 to '44: A Contemporary Memoir*
1945	Voted in the general election. *The Happy Turning, Mind at the End of Its Tether*
1946	Death on 13 August at his home in Hanover Terrace, London

INDEX